CONTEMPLATIVE PRAYER

Contemplative Prayer

A Theology for the Twenty-First Century

JAMES P. DANAHER

 CASCADE *Books* · Eugene, Oregon

CONTEMPLATIVE PRAYER
A Theology for the Twenty-First Century

Cascade Books
An Imprint of Wipf and Stock Publishers
199 W. 8th Ave., Suite 3
Eugene, OR 97401

www.wipfandstock.com

ISBN 13: 978-1-61097-599-5

Cataloging-in-Publication data:

Danaher, James P.

 Contemplative prayer : a theology for the twenty-first century / James P. Danaher.

 xvi + 138 p. ; 23 cm. Includes bibliographical references and index.

 ISBN 13: 978-1-61097-599-5

 1. Spiritual life—Christianity. 2. Mysticism. 3. Christian Life. I. Title.

BV5082.3 D36 2011

Manufactured in the U.S.A.

For Richard Rohr,
His words always made me feel that I was not alone.

Contents

Foreword

FAR TOO FEW OF us understand contemplative prayer. Just this week I asked several Christian leaders to explain it and found they could only take a stab at it. The reasons for this are too numerous to consider here but one reason clearly has to be that our theology of prayer is too small. We have settled for the kind of prayer that is talking to God a great deal. Some of us have added the reading of Scripture into our prayer life. We even have an exegetical method, deeply rooted in the science and philosophy of a modernist hermeneutical system, to guide our reading. The end result is that we have a prayer life that is not the mysterious, love relationship with God that Jesus modeled and calls us to follow.

In *Contemplative Prayer: A Theology for the Twenty-First Century*, Jim Danaher shows us that the kind of prayer that Jesus modeled is a type of prayer that results from having fallen evermore deeply in love with God. Prayer as a mystical, love relationship that transcends words is what genuine followers of Jesus have always understood and such prayer is more appropriate today than ever before. A deep and meaningful prayer life can have no other basis than an ever-deepening love relationship with God. Fall in love with the God that Jesus reveals, and you will have a greater desire to spend time in his presence.

Danaher believes that Jesus' own disciples, as well as all those who have truly followed Jesus over the last two thousand years, have always been people who refused to trust in their own understanding. Universally they have been people who were open to the revelation of Jesus changing their defensive and closed understanding. How does this happen? Danaher believes we must begin with a deep humility (one could say a sanctified doubt) about our own understanding. This means we must perceive how insufficient our first encounter(s) with God really was. This requires a general suspicion of our own understanding of the truth so that we can be genuinely open to having God change our understanding as we come to an ever more fruitful, life-changing, love-driven, interpretation of the one we call the Savior.

Over the course of my Christian life, now nearly six decade long, I have come to agree that it is not so important that I describe, or understand, *how* I entered this journey of faith. It is, however, terribly important that I *continue* this journey as a faithful learner who increasingly knows the mind and heart of Jesus. When I contemplate him in his uniqueness real growth occurs. This growth is not the result of attaining more knowledge of facts but rather one that comes by entering into the *progressive experience* of Jesus' life and teaching. Danaher puts it this way: "The point is not to be right and not make mistakes, but to stay on the journey and allow God to continue to draw us into an ever more fruitful understanding through which to interpret our God experiences."

I first encountered James Danaher in a way that can only be described as divine providence. Browsing in my local bookstore I found his magnificent book, *Eyes That See, Ears That Hear: Perceiving Jesus in a Postmodern Context* (Ligouri/Triumph, 2006). I knew nothing about Danaher but I could not put his book down. Not only did his book powerfully transform my own thinking but I have used it to teach many others who find themselves on this same journey without effective modern guides. What Danaher did was show me why human concepts should not always be trusted. He further showed me how my concepts of love, law, sin, faith, forgiveness, and beauty were all formed through language and some of this language was inadequate, even misleading. He underscored what I had come to see many years ago when I discovered that objective truth was never *purely* objective. What I needed, and my soul so craved, was to fall in love with the Truth—the living, breathing, loving person of Jesus. I soon discovered that a spiritual journey into a more transparent interpretation of the gospel required great faith in the gospel and an equally great distrust of my own understanding.

Now, in *Contemplative Prayer: A Theology for the Twenty-First Century*, Danaher has done it again. This time he has taken my whole being into the love of Jesus, indeed of the whole Trinity. He has shown me that what I genuinely crave is to fall in love with Jesus. I am not even sure that I concur with every interpretation Danaher offers here but I am quite confident he would be fine with this fact. What I am sure of is this; I can never go back to my old way of praying and knowing God because of the sheer beauty and power of this exceedingly fine book.

John H. Armstrong
President of ACT 3 (www.act3online.com) and author of *Your Church Is Too Small: Why Unity in Christ's Mission is Vital to the Future of the Church.*

Acknowledgements

I WOULD LIKE TO acknowledge my many colleagues whose support of my work has been greatly appreciated and valued. I would especially like to acknowledge Michael Scales, President of Nyack College; David Jennings, Executive Vice President of Nyack College; David Turk, Provost of Nyack College; Ronald Walborn, Dean of the Alliance Theological Seminar; and Fernando Arzola, Dean of the College of Arts and Sciences.

Introduction

Prayer and Knowing God

THIS BOOK IS ABOUT prayer, and about how prayer brings us to know God. Most of us do not have a very good idea of prayer nor do we have a good idea of what it means to know God. We think that prayer is about words and knowing God is a matter of believing certain facts about God. Neither is true when we consider either prayer or knowing God on deeper levels.

Guido the Carthusian, a twelfth-century monk, claimed that there were three levels of prayer. The first is all about words and mostly our petitioning God for the things we desire. There is nothing wrong with that but it does not take us very far on the spiritual journey. The second level is that of meditation. This form of prayer is largely a matter of meditating on a Scripture. Often referred to as *Lectio Divina*, it is more about ideas than words. The third level is contemplative prayer and it is about neither words nor ideas but instead is simply a matter of being aware of God's presence and resting in that presence.

As there are levels of prayer, there are likewise levels of knowing. We may know certain facts about a person but that does not mean we know that person. In order to know someone, we must spend time with that person. Think of the celebrities you "know" a lot about but whom you do not know because you have never spent time with them. The same is true of God. Many people "know" and believe certain facts about God, but it is only as we spend time in his presence that we come to know him. Furthermore, the best way to spend time in God's presence is in silence in order that God might commune with us beyond words as lovers often do with a silent gaze. This is the mystery of contemplative prayer.

For most people, prayer is not very mysterious but merely a matter of communing with God through words and ideas. Unfortunately, when prayer is about our words and ideas, we stay in our head, but real prayer—deep prayer—is a thing of the heart. That is because, as we will see, prayer is essentially a matter of being *in love* with God and we do not fall *in love* through our head. As long as we remain in our heads, we are in control, but falling in love is a matter of being out of control.

Being out of control is a scary thing, but that is what we experience when we fall *in love*. We desperately want to be with this other person but we have no control over whether this other person wants to be with us. This is more than a little uncomfortable; it is scary, so we try to gain some control over the other persons love for us. We do this by trying to show the other person how good or beautiful we are. We try to convince them that we behave and think in a way that they will find attractive, and thus they will desire us as much as we desire them. Since falling in love makes this relationship the most important in our lives, we are constantly thinking about how we can continue to attract and thus maintain our relationship with them. This is what keeps us in our head rather than our heart.

Falling in love with God is much the same. As this relationship becomes so important in our lives, we want to have some control over it, so we try to show God that we practice behavior and hold beliefs of which he would approve. We have learned from our experience with human beings that this is how we gain and maintain the affection of those we wish to love us. We hope to control God's affection toward us in a similar way.

In addition to wanting to have some control over God's love toward us, we also usually begin with a certain fear of God as well. Our human experience has taught us that authority is all about using power or the threat of force to make us conform to the will of those in positions of authority. Since God is the ultimate authority, we imagine that he/she wields the greatest threat of force. Thus, being under such an ultimate authority is as frightening as losing the love of the one we fall in love with. Both of these situations are fear producing, but we imagine that we can mitigate the fear with our behavior and beliefs. We can both attract the attention of our lover and appease the possible wrath of some ultimate authority by conforming our behavior and beliefs to their liking.

This is the basis of almost all of religion, and it is where we almost all begin in our relationship with God. The God that Jesus reveals, however, is nothing like what we think or imagine. Unlike human beings, whose love is in response to something good or beautiful in the beloved, the God that Jesus reveals loves all of his creation. He loves all of his children and Jesus tells us that he is even "kind to the ungrateful and the wicked,"[1] and that he "makes his sun rise on the evil and on the good, and sends rain on the righteous and the unrighteous."[2] He neither loves us more for our good behavior or right beliefs nor loves us less for our evil behavior and wrong beliefs. Furthermore, contrary to what almost all Western religions tell us, God is not interested in making us into sinless objects of his love. God is capable of loving us in the midst of our sin through his forgiveness and mercy, and our relationship with him is based upon his forgiveness and mercy *regardless of our behavior or beliefs.*

Consequently, being in a love relationship with God is the ultimate out-of-control relationship, because there is nothing we can do to either increase or diminish God's love toward us. Only when we realize this are we capable of getting out of our heads and into a heart relationship with God. As long as we try to gain some control over either securing God's love or avoiding his wrath, we stay in our heads and have a calculating relationship with God. The spiritual journey to which God calls us is a descent into an *in-love* relationship with God through prayer.

1. Luke 6:35.
2. Matt 5:45.

1

Contemplative Prayer
and the Twenty-First Century

MANY PEOPLE TODAY HAVE come to realize that the human condition in which we find ourselves is much more mysterious than both modern science and modern theology had led us to believe. One of the ambitions of modern science was to eliminate all mystery, and religion in the modern period did little to oppose that ambition. In fact, most modern theologies strove to offer an understanding as objective, certain, and precise as their scientific counterparts.

By the twenty-first century, however, we have become aware of the fact that the kind of understanding that the modern mind sought in both science and religion does not best reflect the reality of our human condition. God, who sees things from the perspective of eternity, may see things in their objective certainty, but *we do not.* We see things from a limited perspective within our time and place. From that perspective, we perceive things with all of the historical, cultural, and linguistic biases that we first acquire at our mother's knee and continue to acquire through our interaction with the socio-cultural world of our experience. Unlike our modern ancestors of the seventeenth and eighteenth centuries who imagined that reason and science could bring us to know objective reality, we now know that our experience is never objective but always filtered through the understanding we bring to our experience.

Immanuel Kant (1724–1804) was the first to explain this filtered or phenomenal nature of our experience. Kant believed that the filters that created the phenomenal world of our experience were innate ideas that constituted a universal mental hardware through which the data of experience was processed. Thus, although filtered, we all, for the most part, experienced the same world. By the twenty-first century, however, we now know that what we bring to our experience is much more than what Kant had imagined. With the nineteenth century, we became aware of historicism and the fact that the understanding by which we process the data of experience is relative to our own historical epoch and changes with the vicissitudes of time. Albert Einstein did not have the same understanding that Isaac Newton had concerning the physical universe, nor do physicists today have the same interpretive understanding Einstein had. A psychologist in the twenty-first century does not believe the same thing that Freud believed at the beginning of the twentieth century. Even people who consider themselves Freudians do not have the same understanding that Freud had less than a hundred years ago. Our understanding changes over time, or at least it should. As we experience the world or a text, anomalies often appear that make it difficult to accept the interpretation we had inherited. Thus, we devise new understandings to overcome the anomalies and, once we do, we settle on a new interpretation.

With the twentieth century and the advent of cultural anthropology and a greater understanding of linguistics, we became increasingly aware of just how relative that understanding was to our culture and language community. We now know that the concepts through which we interpret the data of our experience are not God-given but largely the result of human judgments made within history, culture, and language communities. Even the physical place from which we take in the data of experience alters our interpretation of it, as Albert Einstein convincingly demonstrated by showing the relativity of simultaneity.

Today's science has conceded that our understanding will always be *perspectival* rather than objective, and *probable* rather than certain. We now know that what we claim to know through experience is not merely the result of given data but is largely an interpretation of that data. The world that we experience is phenomenal, or a composite of both the raw data of experience and all of the biases within the understanding through which we interpret that data. None of us possesses a God's-eye view. We are interpretative beings, and human judgments passed on to us through history, culture, and language shape our interpretations. Perhaps other creatures without history, culture, or language interpret the data of their experience through a God-given understanding, but human beings certainly do not. It may have been natural in the past to trust our interpretations and treat them as a given reality, since we do not experience a distinction between the data of our experience and the understanding through which we interpret it. Today, however, we know that our experience is a composite of those two very different elements.

In the past, because we were unaware of this complex nature of human experience, we treated every new insightful interpretation in science or theology as if we had finally arrived at *the truth* rather than simply a new interpretation because of the new understanding we brought to the data of the experience. Today, we have finally conceded that there is no way to know whether our present understanding provides the ultimate interpretation. Religion, for the most part, has been slow to accept this, and many religious people continue to insist that their understanding is objective and certain rather than an interpretation. They claim their interpretation represents objective reality and that God does not change. But it is not that *God* changes—what changes is our understanding of our God-experiences. Just as our interpretation of everything changes with changes in our understanding, so too do our God-experiences change with changes in our understanding.

The theologians of the Reformation and Counter-Reformation believed that the sun went around the earth. That is no longer our interpretation. Our understanding has changed. We now know that the mind is not a *tabula rasa*, and we do not simply record data as given. Thus, people with a twenty-first-century understanding find it hard to believe in theologians who thought that the sun did go around the earth, and whose theologies were the direct result of what they saw in the biblical text. If religion is to have an appeal to people with a twenty-first-century understanding of the human condition, it must offer theologies that are more compatible with our present understanding. Instead of theologies that purport to offer objective certitudes, what we need are perspectives that will allow us to explore our ever-changing understanding of the great mystery that is our relationship to God.

In order to develop such perspectives we need to begin with a suspicion concerning our present understanding and the interpretations it produces. Since we are interpretative beings—though most of us are not as aware of that as we should be—we easily mistake our interpretation of an experience for the data of that experience. This is true of all of our experiences but it is especially true of our God-experiences. Although we are generally quick to assign words and concepts to our God-experiences, they are woefully inadequate to interpret our experience with the divine.

While we have only recently become aware of the hermeneutical or interpretative nature of human experience in general, the true mystic has always been aware of this, at least regarding their God-experience. Because of this, while theologians have been intent upon explaining our relationship to God with words that give concrete meaning to that relationship, the contemplative mystic seems content with simply being present to God, without rushing off to create an interpretation of that experience.

This is the prayer of the contemplative. It is a prayer that distrusts one's own understanding because the mystery of God always goes beyond the words and ideas that make up our understanding and provide our interpretation. For contemplatives, their experience of God's presence is always ineffable, unable to be captured in words, and they know whatever words they do later attribute to those experiences will be different from the experience itself. Long before twenty-first-century minds became aware of the hermeneutical nature of our experience, the contemplative mystics knew that the raw data of their God-experience was very different from whatever interpretation they might assign to it.

Of course, there have always been people who claim to be mystics that are very different from what I am describing. Such people claim that their mystical experience is not mysterious at all. They know exactly what God communicates to them and they suffer no self-doubt concerning whether their interpretation replicates what God communicates. To them, their God-experience and their interpretation of that experience are identical. This, however, is unlike the experience of the contemplative mystic, and it is unlike what we now know to be the human condition. We now know that what we call our experience of the world is really an interpretation of data that we form out of the historical and cultural prejudices that make up such a large part of our understanding. The true mystic has always understood that our communion with an infinite and eternal God will necessarily be inexpressible in terms of finite, temporal words. We may need to record our God-experiences somehow in memory, and that requires that we put our experience into words or images, but the mystic knows that the words and images are always insufficient.

I once heard a story of a man who had a dream and when he awoke, he tried to explain it to his wife. He said it was as if he was a big balloon and God's finger was inside of him. As God's finger pointed and pushed in one direction the balloon went in that direction, and when the finger pointed in another direction, he went in that direction. He then admitted to his wife that that was not what actually happened in the dream. Her response was to ask why he had lied about the dream, especially a dream about God. Of course, it was not that he had lied; it was just that divine communication is otherworldly, but if we wish to share those experiences with other human beings, we must use this-worldly words and ideas.

THE MYSTIC TRADITION

There had always been a mystic tradition that understood just how ineffable our God-experience is, but after the great Spanish mystics of the sixteenth century (e.g., Francisco de Osuna [1497–1541], Teresa of Avila [1515–91], and John of the Cross [1542–91]) there were few noted mystics in the modern period. Apart from Brother Lawrence (circa 1614–91) and Madame Guyon (1648–1717) in the seventeenth century, the modern mind abandoned the mystic tradition as it increasingly sought to eliminate mystery rather than explore it. One exception was the eighteenth-century theologian Jonathan Edwards (1703–58). Although many would not consider Edwards to be a mystic, he, like the mystics, did have an acute understanding of the mysterious nature of our God-experiences.

Edwards was one of the leaders of "The Great Awakening," which swept through the American colonies in the 1730s. During that revival, there was a great dispute over whether the manifestations that were taking place were from God or the imagination of the people involved in the revival. Edwards took the position that they were both; that is, that God was doing something amid the people but it was the understanding that the people brought to those experiences that created their interpretation and reaction. Furthermore, he held that the understanding through which we interpret and react to such divine experiences is always inadequate, since with "truly spiritual sensations, not only is the manner of its coming into the mind extraordinary, but the sensation itself is totally diverse from all that men have, or can have, in a state of nature."[1] Thus, for Edwards, our human understanding, which has its basis in our experience of this world, is ill equipped to interpret and assign a concrete meaning to such an experience. Of course, we do interpret and we have to assign a meaning in order to tie the experience down in our memory, but that interpretation and meaning will always be something other than the data of what we actually experienced.

Today, we know that the way Edwards and the mystics understood their God-experiences is the way we human beings experience everything. Since our conceptual understanding is largely the product of the biases we inherit from our historical, cultural, and linguistic traditions, our interpretation of our experience is very different from the raw data of that experience. Thus, like the mystics, twenty-first-century people are aware of just how biased our interpretation may be. This contemporary insight concerning the hermeneutic nature of our human condition should make us suspicious of our own understanding and the interpretation it yields; therein providing us the kind of humility that a life of following Jesus requires.

What makes followers of Jesus different from most religious people in any age is a humility that comes from not knowing or being suspicious of what they know. In Jesus' day, his followers did not worship their own understanding. Instead, they were open to having their understanding changed by Jesus. Unlike many of the religious people of Jesus' day who were confident in their own understanding, those who became followers of Jesus saw how insufficient their understanding was in the light of what Jesus was revealing. Like those religious people of Jesus' day, many religious people today are not open to the Jesus revelation because they are confident in their own understanding. They suffer no self-doubt and their religious faith amounts to little more than a confidence and pride in their own understanding.

By contrast, the ever-greater experience that God desires to draw us into is possible only if we are able to look to God rather than our own understanding for the security we desire. The philosopher John Dewey said that insecurity is what generates the quest for certainty in both philosophy

---

1. Edwards, *The Religious Affections*, 141.

and religion. Religion often appeals to human insecurity by offering doctrinal certitudes rather than God. Today, however, we have come to realize that certainty is beyond our human reach and its illusion is a poor source of security.

This represents good news for the gospel, since the truth of the gospel was never about giving us certainty concerning our understanding. The truth of the gospel is something that we access through a faith journey that is antithetical to certainty. It is only as we step out in faith into the things to which God calls us that we experience God's faithfulness, but the step is always one taken in uncertainty and with a lack of understanding. Much of modern religion supplanted such a spiritual journey and claimed that faith was simply a matter of believing in the truth of certain sacred doctrines. That is very different from the kind of faith to which the gospel calls us. Jesus never associates faith with a belief in sacred doctrines. Instead of doctrinal beliefs that offer certainty, Jesus simply says, "Follow me."[2] When we do follow him, we discover a God who is very different from what we had anticipated. The Jesus whom religion and theology presents is often very different from the Jesus of the Gospels. The religious Jesus is usually a tribal Jesus who has our values and conforms to our notions of right and wrong. He is a Jesus who will punish evildoers and reward good people who, like ourselves, have believed the right things and practiced the right kind of behavior. That is who we would be if we were God, so we make Jesus into our likeness and ignore all the things he says that are so strange and mysterious. We somehow convince ourselves that he did not really mean that we are to turn the other cheek and love our enemies,[3] that the last are really not first and the first last,[4] and that God is not really "kind to the ungrateful and the wicked."[5] A God who prays for his torturers to be forgiven[6] in order that they might spend eternity with him is simply too foreign to our human understanding. Consequently, we simply imagine a Jesus who fits nicely into our understanding rather than

---

2. Matt 4:19; 8:22; 9:9; 16:24; 19:21; Mark 2:14; 8:34; 10:21; Luke 5:27; 9:23, 59; 18:22; John 1:43; 10:27; 12:26; 13:36; 21:19.

3. Matt 5:38–48.

4. Matt 19:30.

5. Luke 6:35.

6. Luke 23:34.

changing our understanding in order that we might come to know the mystery of God's mercy.

THE MYSTERY OF GOD

The Jesus revelation presents us with a mysterious God who is unlike anything we might have anticipated. What we have always wanted from God is a prescription that we might follow in order to feel secure in our relationship with him. Jesus' teachings, however, leave us realizing that God calls us to something far beyond what we are willing or able to do, and thus, we must all trust in the mystery of God's forgiveness and mercy. Of course, we would much prefer a salvation that was left up to us rather than putting it all in God's hands. Thus, modern theologies offered us the idea of salvation by faith, and faith as a belief in certain doctrines, which put things back in our hands. This is very different from the kind of faith of which Jesus spoke, but it does give people the sense that they are good and have found favor with God by believing the right things.

The gospel that Jesus preached, however, was never about providing a moral or theological prescription for us to follow in order to find favor with God. That might be what religion offers, but Jesus' teachings are re-markably devoid of answers. In fact, of the 183 questions asked of Jesus in the Gospels, he answers only three for sure. Maybe you could stretch that to five depending upon what you consider an answer, but answering five out of 183 questions makes it clear that he was not about giving us an-swers. When asked a question, sometimes Jesus simply refuses to answer, or, at other times, either he asks a question in return or answers a different question from the one asked. By contrast, the business of religion, espe-cially in the modern period, became all about answering the questions instead of leading us into the great mystery that is God.

In a modern world that was all about eliminating mystery, a gospel that promises to lead us into a great mystery does not sell well. With the seventeenth and eighteenth centuries, we became ever more intent on see-ing the things we did not understand as puzzles we could solve rather than mysteries into which we needed to gain insight. Modern science told us that there were no mysteries, and reason, properly applied, could, in time, answer all of our questions. We bought into this thinking, and, as a result, it is not surprising that the great medieval mystic tradition for the most part ended with the modern period.

Mysticism, which sought to gain insight into the mystery of who we are in relationship to God, was not very compatible with a modern mind that sought to eliminate all mystery. By the twenty-first century, however, many people have lost confidence in that modern ambition. The world that Einstein presented us with was much more mysterious than Newton's, and a twenty-first-century understanding of the universe is even more mysterious than Einstein had imagined. Just as we can no longer accept Newton's simplistic mechanical view of the universe, neither can we accept the neat, pat answers to life's questions that early modern theology offered.

Today, Eastern religions are growing in popularity in the West because they offer access to an experience rather than answers that provide us with a sense of certainty. This desire for more than an unrealistic sense of certainty is good news for the gospel, since the gospel calls us to the experience of following Jesus, and we only enter into that experience when our understanding is no longer certain and mere answers no longer satisfy us. In order to enter into the journey to which Jesus calls, we must gain some freedom from the prejudices of our own understanding. The purpose of most of Jesus' teachings are just that; that is, they are intended to break down our understanding in order that we might come to a deeper and more transparent God-experience. If taken seriously, the Jesus revelation should destabilize our understanding and therein free us to encounter the radically divine God that Jesus reveals.

Jesus' first and longest teaching is the Sermon on the Mount. It covers three full chapters at the beginning of the first of the four Gospel accounts. In it, Jesus tells us that nearly everything we think is wrong. We think that adultery is a sin, but Jesus tells us that mere lust is just as sinful as adultery. We think that murder is sinful, but he tells us that anger is equivalent to murder. Even things that we find praiseworthy, like making and keeping our oaths, Jesus condemns. Jesus condemns other things that we see as praiseworthy as well. He condemns worry, but we think worry is a good thing—it means we are responsible, and being responsible is a good thing, or so we imagine. He condemns judgments, but we think we have to pass judgments. He even tells us that we cannot love earthly treasure but we must love our enemies. He is turning our world upside down and destabilizing our understanding. We want a god who loves good people and punishes bad people. The last thing we want is a God who is "kind to the ungrateful and the wicked."[7] We want Jesus to confirm the prejudices that make up our understanding in order that we might feel secure in those prejudices, but instead Jesus is destroying our understanding in order to draw us into the mystery that is the mercy of God.

OUR JOURNEY INTO THE MYSTERY

A journey motif runs throughout the Bible. God calls Abraham to a journey into an unknown land, Moses leads the people on a journey to a Promised Land that none of them had ever seen, and Jesus says, "Follow me" and leads us into a similar spiritual journey. A journey into the unknown, however, is exactly what we do not want. We find certitudes comforting, and modernity told us we were right to desire certainty. In fact, the founders of modernity equated certainty with truth after the model of mathematics. This makes it very difficult to understand the truth to which Jesus calls us. Jesus tells us that he is "the way and the truth and the life"[8] but such a truth—which is the way of life that Jesus reveals—is not what we want. We much prefer a truth that provides our understanding with a sense of certainty, and religion is generally very accommodating. Instead of calling us to a journey, religion tells us that there is no journey or that the journey can be over in an instant by simply buying into the beliefs, rituals, or practices that they offer. Religion usually gives us just what we want, and provides our understanding with explanations that make sense and give us something to hold onto. That, however, is the very thing that keeps us from the journey to which Jesus calls us. Religion gives us a way to avoid the journey into the infinitely knowable mystery that is God by telling us that it is no mystery at all, and that if we trust the doctrines they set forth, we will know all we need to know about God.

This is the great heresy. We constantly fall into believing that because we know certain truths about God, our knowing puts us in a privileged place with God from which we are no longer in need of mercy but have been made righteous by what we know. The journey into the mystery of God, however, is never about what we know, but rather about deeper

7. Luke 6:35.
8. John 14:6.

and deeper experiences of God's mercy and forgiveness. According to Christian orthodoxy, Satan would know all the truths of the church but he does not seek the experience of God's mercy and forgiveness. Many religious people take on a similar nature when they think that because they know something *about* God, they are righteous and no longer need to experience God's mercy. Believing that they know, and they know with certainty, comforts them and gives them a sense of security. Consequently, they accept the certitudes of religion and settle for that sense of certainty rather than following Jesus into the mystery. This is where nearly all of us begin, and maybe it is a necessary starting point, but ultimately we find that our own understanding is a poor source of security. Hopefully, we eventually come to realize that the security we seek comes from the experience of God's presence and not our own understanding. That experience is the ultimate form of prayer, and we enter into that prayer by leaving our understanding behind and experiencing the mystery of God's presence. It is a mystery because, as we have said, it is ineffable and always beyond whatever words we assign to it.

Our first encounter with such a presence often occurs when we no longer find security in what we know. At those times when the understanding through which we interpret the world becomes destabilized, we enter into what the mystic refers to as "the dark night of the soul." In the dark night of the soul, the sense you were always able to make of the world is gone, and the security your understanding had always provided has evaporated. It is a little like being a child again. Remember how scary some things were because you had not figured anything out yet? Without their understanding to count on, children depend upon their parents, but when adult understanding breaks down all we can count on is God and the sense that he has us and we are safe in his presence. When we sense that, it is better than all the understanding we could ever imagine.

Of course, the false sense of certainty that our understanding provides is always initially more attractive than the certainty that God provides because it is something that we can possess rather than something that possesses us. This is why we are so attracted to theology, and the more certain the theology the better. Not that theology is bad. Surely, we need some theology. When, however, we imagine that our theology provides a perfect or even adequate understanding of an infinite and eternal God, our theology becomes the thing that keeps us from the ever-greater intimacy to which God calls us. In such cases, our theology becomes the idol that we look to for our sense of security rather than God. This is why the dark night of the soul is so essential. If our understanding is not destabilized, we will never seek security apart from that understanding. Why would we? If our understanding provides all the certainty and security we need, why would we seek security anywhere else? That is why so much of Jesus' teaching is about destabilizing our understanding. Jesus, however, does not simply destabilize our understanding and leave us there. He says, "Follow me" and leads us into the mystery. He is the way, but the way is not a theological way through which we might gain an evermore-certain understanding of God, but rather a path of prayer through which we might experience our union with God.

This might seem a little strange at first since Jesus' teachings on what we call prayer are rather limited in comparison to his teachings on things like forgiveness or the evils of wealth and hypocrisy, but that is because we have a very limited, cultural notion of prayer being all about words. Prayer, as we will continually see throughout this book, is simply a matter of being aware of God's presence and, as such, Jesus' entire life was a prayer. Jesus prayed without ceasing, and what is most essential about following him and living as he lived is that we too pray without ceasing.

When we think about following Jesus and doing what he did, however, we would much prefer to raise the dead and give sight to the blind. God using us to perform miracles would make us feel great, but practicing an awareness of God's presence has the opposite effect: it makes us realize that we are not very spiritual. When we try to practice an awareness of God's presence, we are quickly humbled and immediately convinced that we are not very good at being attentive to God. We are distracted from an awareness of God's presence by just about anything. Unlike Jesus, whose love-relationship with the Father kept him in a constant state of awareness of his Father's presence, we constantly drift off into all sorts of other concerns that capture and possess our attention. The good news, however, is that it is this recognition of our failure to give God the kind of attention that love demands that causes us to repent or turn our attention back toward God. When we do, we experience forgiveness, and as we become evermore aware of our sin of not giving God the attention that love requires, we find ourselves in an almost constant state of receiving forgiveness.

We might at first think that living in an almost perpetual state of repentance, and being the constant recipient of forgiveness, is hardly the Christian ideal. We want to do it right, and repentance means we are doing it wrong, but to borrow Richard Rohr's great line, "We come to God not by doing it right but by doing it wrong." Indeed, the gospel is all about the forgiveness of sins, but what we do not seem to get is that God extends forgiveness toward us and sanctifies us through his forgiveness in order to make us, not into his sinless likeness, but rather into his forgiving and merciful likeness. Religion tells us that God wants us to be sinless, but Jesus tells us that "he who has been forgiven little loves little."[9] The gospel is all about bringing us into a deeper understanding and experience of God's forgiveness in order that we would become the body of Christ and bring his forgiveness and mercy to the world. The means to that deeper understanding and experience is the kind of prayer we will be discussing throughout this text.

9. Luke 7:47 NIV.

2

Contemplative Prayer as Being in Love with God

THE SPANISH PHILOSOPHER, JOSE Ortega y Gasset (1883–1955) said, "Falling in love, initially, is no more than this: attention abnormally fastened upon another person."[1] It certainly seems true that "For the lover his beloved . . . possesses a constant presence,"[2] and occupies the lover's attention in a way that nothing else can. What is so noticeable about people in love is that they have their attention abnormally fixed upon one another, but I think this idea of attention abnormally fixed is not limited to romantic love. Attention is at the base of most, if not all, forms of love, and it is what we most desire in terms of someone loving us. The affection children desire from their parents largely involves attention, in the same way that the affection we desire in a romantic relationship largely involves attention. Even the love that exists between friends requires that we are capable of fixing our attention upon our friend, and if someone that we consider a friend is unwilling to give us her attention, we feel we may have been mistaken in considering her a friend in the first place.

Unfortunately, as much as we desire the attention of spouses, parents, or friends, we human beings are not very good at fixing our attention on

1. Ortega y Gasset, *On Love*, 64.
2. Ibid. 65.

anything for very long.[3] Because of this, we are a constant disappointment to those who desire our love. If we understand love in terms of attention, then our love is certainly fleeting, even concerning the things we love most. Indeed, if we measure love by our ability to fix our attention on the ones we love, then the vast majority of human beings make poor lovers. Indeed, we are often disappointed by, and a disappointment to, those we love most. The reason other human beings fail to be attentive to us, and we fail to be attentive to them, is because we are easily distracted by almost anything and find it very difficult to be present and attentive. Our search for a lover who will give us the extraordinary attention we desire is not completely frustrated, however, since there is one who is ever present and attentive.

God's omnipresent and omniscient nature makes him the supreme lover and the only one who can truly satisfy our desire for the kind of attention that human beings always fail to provide one another. God is one whose "eyes will be open" and his "ears attentive,"[4] and "like an eagle that stirs up its nest and hovers over its young,"[5] he will attend to us as "the apple of his eye."[6] This attention, which God alone can satisfactorily provide, is not, however, merely the result of God's omnipresent nature. God's nature makes him aware and present to the whole of his creation, but the focus of his love or attention is upon a race of beings that he desires to make into his forgiving and merciful likeness. He accomplishes this not through power or might but through his mere presence and the attentive love that he extends toward us. Sadly, many people never experience his presence and spend lives oblivious of the attention he extends toward us. That is because we only experience his presence in prayer.

We may associate prayer with words or ideas about God, but prayer is ultimately about our awareness of God being present and attentive to us. Whenever we are aware of God's presence, we are in a state of prayer; and whenever we are not aware of his presence, we are not in prayer, regardless of the words we may be mumbling. Furthermore, it is only when prayer becomes such an experience that we realize the love that our parents, spouses, and friends were so unable to supply.

3. Ibid. 62–63.
4. 2 Chr 7:15, NIV.
5. Deut 32:10–11, NIV.
6. Zech 2:8, NIV.

Prayer is the ultimate blessing God has for us, since nothing compares to the experience of his presence. Likewise, prayer is all that God desires from us. Contrary to what we have been told about God requiring that we conduct the right rituals, believe the right things, or behave in the right way, all God really desires is that we become aware of his attentive presence and respond to it with our own attentive presence. There is a great story about this in Luke's Gospel. Martha is busy doing all the things that she thinks will please Jesus, while her sister Mary chooses to sit at Jesus' feet and be present and attentive to him. That is the only thing that God desires: that we be present and attentive to him. Jesus tells Martha that she is "worried and distracted by many things,"[7] and that Mary has chosen the only thing that is important.[8]

God's desire is that we would be present and attentive to him as he is present and attentive to us. Indeed, our love toward God is essentially a matter of attention just as his love toward us is largely a matter of attention. We love God to the extent that God is in all our thoughts and we are attentive to his presence. Just as children measure the love of their parents by the amount and quality of the attention they receive from them, and wives measure the love of their husbands by their attention, we can measure our love toward God by attention as well. When we do, we should immediately see how little we love God in comparison to God's great love for us.

LOVING GOD WITH YOUR WHOLE HEART

When one of the scribes asked Jesus what was the greatest commandment, Jesus tells him, "You shall love the Lord your God with all your heart, and with all your soul, and with all your mind, and with all your strength."[9] If love is essentially a matter of attention, then loving God with all of our heart, soul, mind, and strength means that we are aware of God and attentive to his presence in all that we do. This is exactly the righteousness that Jesus modeled for us. He did not seek a right relationship with God by observing holy days or avoiding the company of sinners. Neither did he avoid behavior that the religious people of his day saw as sinful. What he

7. Luke 10:41.

8. Luke 10:38–42.

9. Mark 12:30.

did do, however, was maintain an awareness of God's presence in all that he did; that is, he loved God with all of his heart, soul, mind, and strength in a way that we never do. Unlike us, Jesus entire life was a prayer and he constantly fixed his attention upon God's presence in his life.

Such a life certainly represents the greatest degree of affection for God. In our culture, we understand degrees of affection. The word "like" connotes a normal degree of affection, while the word "love" connotes a greater degree of affection. When we wish to express a still greater degree of affection, we say that we do not merely love the other person but that we are in love with them. Likewise, when someone wants to express the fact that she does not have the ultimate degree of affection for someone, we might hear her say, "I love you, but I'm not in love with you."

To be in love with someone implies, not just affection, but a desire for an intimacy that goes beyond what we have with people we merely like or even love. When we are in love, we desire a relationship that cuts "beneath the roles and functions in terms of which [we] ordinarily comport [ourselves] toward others."[10] When we are in love, we seek a relationship that goes deeper than any other relationship—a relationship in which we "relate to [our] beloved as she is in her uniqueness behind roles and masks."[11] It is an intimacy that we hope will bring us into a union whereby we will "participate in an intimate common life with another self."[12] This is just the kind of love-relationship God desires to establish with us. Jesus modeled just such a relationship for us, and it is what it means to love God with all our heart, soul, mind, and strength. We may experience such an in-love relationship with God when we are in states of deep prayer and become aware of his presence and the sense of a shared life, but such experiences are usually only momentary. In no time, the distractions set in and the focus of our attention takes us somewhere else. It is at these moments, however, that we realize how ill-equipped we are for a genuine love-relationship with God and how our love-relationship with God will always be in need of his forgiveness. None of us has the kind of relationship with God that Jesus modeled, and we all must trust that God will maintain our love-relationship with him through his forgiveness

10. Ehman, "Personal Love," 255.

11. Ibid.

12. Ibid., 254.

and mercy. This alone puts us in right relationship with God, and being in a right relationship with God is exactly what it means to be righteous.

Many people who consider themselves Christians do not understand righteousness in such a way. They imagine that through their rituals, beliefs, or behavior they have become sinless, and God can now love them because they are sinless rather than simply forgiven. Some may even believe that they do love God with all of their heart, soul, mind, and strength, but that to do so they must completely ignore the life that Jesus modeled and calls us to follow.

As we have said, Jesus' entire life was a prayer. He was always aware of another presence other than his own, and was never distracted from an awareness of the divine presence the way we so easily are by almost anything. Jesus perfectly modeled a life of "attention abnormally fastened"[13] upon God, and therein he showed us how to share a common life with God. He says, "I am *in* the Father and the Father is *in* me" (my italics).[14] This in-love relationship whereby two individuals fix their attention upon one another and come to share a common life is the life that Jesus models and calls us to follow.

We balk at this and quickly point out that Jesus was the Son of God; that Jesus and the Father were one, and therefore we cannot hope to have the same relationship with God that Jesus had. Jesus, however, does not simply tell us that God is *his* father, but that God is *our* father as well. Throughout the Gospels, Jesus refers to God as either "*our* father," "*your* father," "*your* heavenly father," or "*your* father in heaven" twenty-seven times.[15] This is the blasphemy that some religious people of Jesus day found so upsetting. Saying that God was one's own father was impious to some of the religious people of Jesus' day and many religious types today still see it as impious.

Of course, believing that the God of the universe is our own father can have the detrimental effect of making us feel special and favored by God. If someone sees her- or himself as God's beloved daughter or son, they can easily think they are special in God's sight, which can and often does fill them with arrogance rather than the love of God. Jesus, however,

13. Ortega y Gasset, *On Love*, 64.

14. John 14:10.

15. Matt 5:16, 45, 48; 6:1, 4, 6, 8–9, 14–15, 18, 26, 32; 7:11; 10:20, 29; 18:14, 35; Mark 11:25; Luke 6:36; 10:21; 11:13; 12:30, 32; 15:21; John 8:41; 20:17.

tells us that God is a father who loves the prodigal son as much as the good son,[16] and that God's love for us has nothing to do with something special about us but something special about God. God loves all of his children and wants nothing more than that they would be present with him. He wants the prodigal to return from his wanderings and be present with him, just as he wants the older, good son to be present with him at the party he is throwing for his younger son.[17] Throughout Jesus teachings, we see the non-preferential nature of God's love. Indeed, what Jesus' teachings ultimate reveal is that we are all prodigals who have left our father's presence and gone off to find life and meaning in the many distractions that this world provides; and the only good thing we can do is to return to an awareness of his presence through repentance. Thus, although we are God's beloved, it is not because of something special about *us*. We are all prodigals, and our love-relationship with God will always rest upon his forgiveness and mercy.

FORGIVENESS AND MERCY

Certainly, God could have made us attentive creatures with a greater capacity for love and less proclivity for distraction. If he had, however, although we would have had a greater capacity for love, it would not have been God's kind of love. God loves through forgiveness and mercy, and his purpose behind creation was not to create people that would love and be attentive to him but to create beings that would love *as he loves*. In order to make us into being after his likeness, capable of loving as he loves, God created a people with limited capacity for love, but a great capacity for receiving forgiveness, so that by receiving much forgiveness we would eventually become forgiving creatures ourselves. We only become forgiving by being forgiven much, and "the one to whom little is forgiven loves little."[18] Thus, we become forgiving creatures after God's likeness not by doing it right but by doing it wrong.

Sadly, religious people are always trying to come to God by doing it right, but Jesus is constantly trying to show us that we do not do it right and must depend upon God's forgiveness and mercy. God's purpose of

16. Luke 15:11–32.
17. Ibid.
18. Luke 7:47, ISV.

making us into his forgiving and merciful likeness is only realized when we become aware of this and begin to open ourselves to the experience of the forgiveness God constantly extends toward us. In order for us to become forgiving, as he is forgiving, it is not enough that God forgives us, but we must become aware of that forgiveness. Have you ever been hurt and forgiven someone without them ever realizing the offense or your forgiveness? You may have forgiven them but they never experienced forgiveness. The same is certainly true of God. We are generally oblivious of the way we offend God and the forgiveness God constantly extends to us. To become aware of it, we need to realize how much we fail to be in love with God as he is in love with us, and how, in spite of our failure, God continues to extend his forgiving presence to us. As we become evermore aware of this experience of his forgiveness, we become more like him regarding forgiveness and therein become agents capable of loving as he loves.

This is the most undesirable part of following Jesus. We love the idea of following him in order to go to heaven, and we are even OK with doing miracles in his name, but forgiveness means that we must suffer the offense of others in order to restore relationship with them. Why would we want to restore relationship with those who offend us? It has no natural appeal to us and God must build it into us through the experience of being the perpetual recipient of his forgiveness. Becoming aware of the fact that we are the object of God's love may come in an instant; becoming agents of God's love is quite another matter. In order to become like him regarding forgiveness and mercy we need to live in an almost constant state of repentance, since repentance is the very thing that makes us aware of God's forgiveness and without it his forgiveness goes unnoticed.

Unfortunately, many of us do not have a very good understanding of repentance. We imagine that if we have not murdered anyone or committed adultery we have no need of repentance, but Jesus tells us that the great commandment is to love God with all of our heart, soul, mind, and strength; that is, that we are to be in love with God. Such an in-love relationship is not damaged only when we commit murder or adultery but simply when we fail to give God the kind of attention that being in love demands. Since we constantly fail to be in love with God as he is in love with us, God's forgiveness must constantly sustain the relationship. This is a central theme of Jesus' teachings. He constantly points out that our sin is much greater than we think and so too is our need for repentance in order that we might experience God's forgiveness.

The Greek word that the New Testament translates as repentance is *metanoia*: literally to "rethink" or "change your mind." This changing of the mind that is repentance is a matter of turning our attention back toward God and away from all the distractions that keep us from an awareness of his presence. This is the nature of repentance and it should become an ever-greater part of our lives as we continue to consider the relationship with God that Jesus models for us. If we seriously consider following Jesus into the kind of life to which he calls us, it should be obvious that we are not very good at living in a constant awareness of God's presence, as Jesus had. We have our attention diverted from an awareness of God's presence by just about anything. Our failure to give God the attention that an in love-relationship demands, however, should cause us to continually turn back in repentance to the awareness of his presence that is prayer.

Of course, even if we were capable of giving God the kind of attention that being in love requires, and lived in a constant state of prayer, we would still fall short of an in love-relationship with God. That is because being in love also requires an intimate knowing concerning the other person. Without truly knowing the other person, we are in love with an illusion rather than who that person really is. When we seek to be in love and share a common life with an infinite, eternal, and divine person, what we can know of that person is certainly limited. In spite of all of the revelations that God offers, we receive those revelations into a finite and temporal human understanding. Thus, God will always be something of a mystery to us, and our love-relationship with God will always be something that we pursue through a mysterious journey into a deeper knowing. As mysterious as that knowing is, however, it is something we can know through prayer and the practice of his presence.

As we have said, the last thing that religious people want is a journey into an infinitely knowable mystery. What most want are certitudes concerning what we must *do* to manipulate God in order to gain heaven and avoid hell. We thus create theologies that eliminate mystery and give us the kind of absolute certainty we desire. We then call our belief in such theologies, "faith." In so doing, we completely miss the radically divine nature of the Jesus revelation. What Jesus reveals is that God is not like the theological idols that we create in order to convince ourselves that

God finds favor with us because of our rituals, beliefs, or behaviors. Jesus tells us just the opposite: that no one finds favor and all must depend upon God's forgiveness and mercy.

Jesus shows us what it means to love God "with all your heart, and with all your soul, and with all your mind, and with all your strength,"[19] by living in a constant state of prayer or attentiveness to God's presence. This is what we have been describing as being in love with God. Prayer, like being in love, is a matter of attention abnormally fixed, and Jesus lived his entire life in such a prayerful, in-love relationship with God. We fail to live the kind of life that Jesus modeled. Almost anything distracts us from an awareness of God's presence, but there, hidden in our sin, is the good news. The good news is that any time we repent of the distractions that so easily possess us, and return to an awareness of his presence, we are the recipients of his forgiveness and mercy, which is always greater than our sin. This repeated experience of his forgiveness eventually makes us evermore into his forgiving likeness. Thus, we take on his likeness and become the angelic agents of his forgiveness and mercy, not by doing it right, but by realizing that we do it wrong. Two thousand years after Jesus first preached this gospel, most who consider themselves Christians still do not get it.

19. Mark 12:30.

3

Prayer as Presence

As WE SAW IN the last chapter, both prayer and being in love are largely a matter of attention. Furthermore, we only come to know God as we fix our attention upon him and spend time in his presence. That is because the way we come to know a person, especially a divine person, is different from the way we come to know a thing or object. Personal knowledge is always revelatory. That is, the person we wish to know must reveal themselves and what they think, feel, or believe. Thus, with personal knowledge the knower is somewhat powerless. God may know our deepest thoughts because of his omniscient nature, but we only come to know another person, be they human or divine, by their choosing to reveal themselves to us. Of course, we do have a part in the revelation in that we must put ourselves in a place to receive what they wish to reveal. If we wish to know a human being, we must put ourselves in a place of being attentive to her or him. The same is true if we wish to know God. We must put ourselves in a place of prayer or being attentive to whatever God might want to reveal.

Most of us, however, do not conceive of prayer as being attentive to God. That is because our concept of prayer does not come from what Jesus models in the Gospels, but from our parents and other adult members of our culture and language community. Their idea of prayer centers on words. As children, our parents told us to *say* our prayers. The pastor says, "let us pray" and words follow. We come to think that prayer is all about words. One day when I was at a prayer meeting, there was a short silence before we began to pray. Before a minute had passed one of the men blurted out, "If we're not going to pray, I have better things to do." Our culture has led us to believe that prayer is all about words, but Jesus seems to suggest that the heart of prayer is not about words. He says, "When you are praying, do not heap up empty phrases as the Gentiles do; for they think they will be heard because of their many words. Do not be like them, for your Father knows what you need before you ask him."[1] The fact that Jesus says, "your father knows what you need before you ask" certainly seems to make the point that God does not need words to understand our heart. Augustine reinforces the point that the words we use in prayer are not necessary in order for us to communicate with God, since God knows our hearts and is not in need of the medium of words. "When we pray there is no need of speech, that is of articulate words, except perhaps as priests use words to give a sign of what is in their minds, not that God may hear, but that men may hear and, being put in remembrance, may with some consent be brought into dependence on God."[2]

Paul also implies the same thing when he says, "pray without ceasing."[3] It seems obvious that Paul does not expect us to be constantly mumbling words. Someone once asked Mother Teresa what she said when she prayed. She responded by saying that she did not say anything, but she listened. When then asked what God said when she listened, she said, "He doesn't say anything, he listens." God listening to us listen to him. What a beautiful picture of prayer. It is like two lovers simply enjoying one another's presence without saying a word. If this is a picture of prayer, then some people never pray in spite of their mumbling words that they call prayers, while other people live lives of prayers, although saying little. What is essential to prayer is neither words nor silence but presence. That is, we need to be present to God as God is present to us.

What it means to be present is that we are here and nowhere else. To achieve true communication with any person, human or divine, we must be present to that other person. Today many people find it extremely difficult to be present. In contrast to past ages, our modern, postindustrial culture requires a great deal of planning if we are to be successful. To succeed in our world today, we have to focus upon the future rather than

1. Matt 6:7–8 NRSV.

2. Augustine, *De Magistro*, 70.

3. 1 Thess 5:17.

merely the here and now. The further we wish to climb the ladder of success, the more we need to plan and be looking to the next thing we have to do. Because of this, successful people tend to live in the future, and their attention is always somewhere else and seldom here and now. For many successful people who are constantly planning the next thing they have to do, it is very difficult to be present enough to have truly intimate relationships.

There are other people, who, although not possessed by thoughts of the future, experience a different problem. They are seldom present because things in the past, either good or bad, possess their attention and keep them from being present. In order to be capable of genuine personal relationships, with either human beings or God, we must be present and escape the pull of both past and future.

The book of Genesis tells us that Adam walked with God in the Garden. Of course, God has never ceased to walk with us but we have lost our awareness of his presence. He is still present to us but we are not present to him. This is our great sin. What grieves God is our lack of desire to be present to him and live in an awareness of him being present to us. That is, we do not live lives of prayer as Jesus had.

PRAYER AS EXPERIENCING THE OMNIPRESENCE OF GOD

In contrast to human beings, who have great difficulty being present, God is omnipresent. The omnipresence of God is widely attested to in Scripture. The Psalmist David says, "Where can I go from your spirit? Or where can I flee from your presence? If I ascend to heaven, you are there; if I make my bed in Sheol, you are there."[4] Likewise, Jeremiah says, "Am I a God near by, says the Lord, and not a God far off?"[5]

Of course, it is one thing to believe in the omnipresence of God as a theory and another to experience the omnipresence of God. What Jesus knew, and constantly sensed, was an awareness of his Father's presence. That same presence is available to us. Since God is omnipresent, all we need to do in order to sense his presence is to be present ourselves. Sadly, we are seldom present, and our minds constantly lead us off into concerns for the future or memories of the past. We are seldom here now, but when

4. Ps 139:7–8.

5. Jer 23:23.

we do manage to be present, we are having a God-experience; whether we recognize it as such or not is another matter.

God abides not in the past or future but in his omnipresence, and whenever we enter into the present, we enter into God's realm. When we are present, we are no longer in our heads but have entered God's eternal present and it is only there that we can become aware of another conscious besides our own. When we occupy our minds with thought of the future or the past, we are in our own world where there is no room for anything but our own consciousness. When we are present, however, and refuse to be possessed by thought of the future or past, we open ourselves to another consciousness not our own. All the mystics attest to this fact that by being present they are able to become aware of a deeper consciousness. In fact, it is a consciousness so deep that it feels as if it is not our own, although we feel somehow deeply connected to it, as if it were part of us.

This is what the mystic senses. It is the sense that when I am able to be present in prayer, I become aware of another consciousness deeper than my own, yet so present and attentive to me that it feels as if it is a part of me or I am a part of it. "My deepest me is God" is a line attributed to both Meister Eckhart (1260–1327) and Catherine of Genoa (1447–1510), but probably represents the sentiments of hosts of other mystics as well. This awareness of another consciousness being aware of us is not like being aware of a physical presence the way we are aware of the furniture around us. We may sense that other people are aware of our physical presence, but it is different when we sense another person being aware of, and present to, our conscious state. When we sense that another person is present to our conscious state and is focusing their attention upon us and our circumstances in the way we focus upon ourselves and our circumstances, we get the sense that we are not alone.

We all suffer from loneliness and we only overcome that sense of being alone by experiencing the presence of another consciousness extending attention and good will toward us. A great deal of the healing and sense of well-being that comes through psychotherapy is simply the result of our becoming aware of another person giving their attention and being present to our circumstances and the way we uniquely experience those circumstances. Only this can overcome the loneliness from which we all suffer, and it is this that we hope for in our relationships with parents, spouses, and the best of friends. Sadly, some of us are without such human contact, and others of us are insensitive to it even when there is such a human presence. What is most sad, however, is the fact that nearly all of us are insensitive to the one that is always present. We are never alone, although most of us go through our lives unaware of God's constant presence. Most of us fail to experience the omnipresence of God and instead merely acknowledge it as an abstract idea or theory, if we acknowledge it at all. In contrast to how oblivious we are to the experience of God's omnipresence, Jesus lived his entire life in that experience. When Jesus calls us to follow him, his desire is that we too would constantly sense God's presence, just as he had.

This experience of God's omnipresence is considerably different from what I hear many Christians refer to as the experience of "the manifest presence of God." Today, many Christians claim to experience a manifest presence of God that is different from the omnipresence of God. Their claim is that at times God manifests his presence and is more present than usual. Some contemporary revivalists have described it as God being especially present in a particular place or time, or as God being "here more than there."[6] In other words, "God chooses to concentrate or reveal himself more strongly in one place than another, or more at one time than another."[7] That seems a rather strange and extremely anthropocentric view of God. Certainly, God can call attention to his presence just as we could call attention to our presence. Imagine yourself at a party where you do not know many people. You could draw attention to your presence by shouting in your loudest voice. Suddenly everyone would be aware of your presence, but even before your shout, there may have been people at the party that were aware of your presence without your shouting. The same is true of our awareness of God's presence. At times God may do something in order to draw our attention to his presence, but it is not as though he becomes more present than he was previously. He is always there and it is a matter of our awareness as to whether we recognize his presence. Some are only aware of the shouts that reveal God's presence, but others are aware of his presence even when God does not shout. God is omnipresent, and part of what that entails is that he cannot be more present than he already is.

6. Tenney, *The God Chasers*, 37.
7. Ibid.

We might be right to speak of human beings being more or less present. As we have said, being present is essentially a matter of having our attention focused on the here and now rather than somewhere else, and human beings are not very good at being present. That, however, is not the case with God. God's attention does not increases and decreases the way human attention does, and he cannot be more present than he already is. The truth is that when we speak of God manifesting his presence, we are not referring to an increase in God's attention toward us but rather an increase in our attention toward God. It is not that God becomes more present to us, but that we become more present to God.

One of the reasons that we so easily slip into a wrong understanding of our God-experience and imagine that God is more present in certain places than others is because we had for so long believed that the mind was something of a tabula rasa that merely recorded objective reality as given. Today, we know that our experience is more complex and the result of both what we receive through the senses, and how we interpret that data through the understanding we have inherited from our history, culture, and language community. Our God-experiences are no different. They are always a composite of what God communicates and how we interpret that communication. It is never easy to sort out what we bring to the experience in the form of our understanding from what we receive in the experience from God—many people do not even try. They naively imagine that we simply record objective reality. I hear people say, "I know what they said!" as if our interpretation and the speakers intent were identical. They believe that the way things appear to them is the way things objectively are. They are unaware of any difference between the two, so they imagine that what they experience is objective reality. That is as naïve as believing that water is not made up of two very different elements (hydrogen and oxygen) because we do not experience water that way.

Concerning our God-experience, the reality is that God is omnipresent, but it may appear to us that God shows up at times, but not at other times. That is our interpretation—the way things appear to us and not the way things are. What we refer to as an experience of God's manifest presence is certainly very real, but it is an apparent reality. The ultimate reality, beyond our interpretation, is that God is *always* present. Since we only become aware of that presence at certain times or under certain conditions, we imagine that God has finally decided to show up. Of course, we are the ones that have finally showed up or become attentive and present to God's omnipresence. God certainly may do something that specifically draws our attention to his presence, but that certainly does not mean that he was absent or less than present before that. God is always present—he is not the one who comes and goes. God's presence does not wane, and what we call the manifest presence of God is psychological, or a matter of our becoming aware of God's presence. The fact that God appears more present at certain times or in certain places is a matter of our psychological state concerning the degree to which we are aware of his presence—perhaps as a result of divine action by which God calls attention to his presence—but not a matter of God actually being more present.

It should not be surprising that people are more aware of God's presence in contemplative prayer or worship, since prayer and worship have the specific intention of making us sensitive to God's presence. Unfortunately, we too easily imagine that when we enter into prayer or worship God responds with his presence: that our prayer or worship is what causes God to show up. Nothing could be further from the truth. It may seem that we need to pray or worship before God decides to show up, but the truth is that we are constantly distracted and insensitive to God's presence, except for those rare occasions in prayer or worship. Even in our prayer and worship, it often takes a long time to sense God's presence, but that is because we take a long time to free ourselves from all the distractions that keep us from an awareness of his presence. It is certainly not because God takes a long time to decide to reveal his presence.

In the past, it may have been easy to believe that we were attentive to God's presence in prayer or worship, and that God was hiding himself from us or choosing not to be present for some reason. In the past, it was equally easy for people to believe that the sun went around the earth, but the sun does not go around the earth in spite of what we think we see, and God does not hide himself from us. It may seem that the sun is moving and not the earth. That is the way it appears to us. Likewise, it may seem that we are attentive and God is not there, but that is merely our perspective. God is always there and we are distracted by just about anything, and therefore, many of us only become aware of God's presence with the spectacular or miraculous. This is why Jesus tells us, "An evil and adulterous generation seeks after a sign."[8] An evil and adulterous generation seeks

8. Matt 16:4.

signs or wonders because they have no prayer life or experience of God presence apart from the spectacular.

This is not to deny or downplay the miraculous or spectacular. God is certainly present in what we call the manifest presence of God, but it is a matter of our perspective to think that he is present at that moment in a way that is different from the way he is always present. God is not present in the miraculous in a greater way than he is present in the "still small voice."[9] Our belief that the miraculous represents a greater presence is the result of both our cultural prejudice, which favors the spectacular, and the fact that we are dull to the experience of his omnipresence. Since few of us practice experiencing the omnipresence of God, our only experience with his presence is in terms of the miraculous, but this is very different from the life that Jesus modeled for us.

Jesus was aware that the Father and the Spirit were as present with him in his times of eating with his disciples as when he was raising the dead or giving sight to the blind. If we are to follow him and live as he lived, we need to be aware of God's omnipresence the way Jesus was constantly aware. For Jesus there was no difference in his awareness of God's presence from one situation to the next: whether the situation was miraculous or mundane was irrelevant. Furthermore, part of the good news that Jesus brings is that we can live in the awareness of God's presence just as Jesus had. Of course, our awareness of God's presence will not be as perfect as Jesus' awareness. Our failure to live as Jesus lived, however, is the very thing that should keep us in an almost constant state of repentance, which brings us back into that awareness and the experience of God's forgiveness and mercy.

As we have said, following Jesus is not about doing it right but about realizing that we do it wrong. We constantly drift from an awareness of God's presence, in a way that Jesus never did, but an awareness of that is what causes us to turn back or repent, and once again become aware of the forgiveness through which he always provides access to his presence. It is our recognition of our failure to live as Jesus lived, in a constant awareness of God's presence, which brings us to repentance and the experience of God's forgiveness, the repeated experience of which makes us into forgiving people.

9. 1 Kgs 19:12.

This is what distinguishes the saint from the rest of us. While most understand their need to repent for their acts of murder or adultery, the saint repents for not having been sensitive to God's presence. Thus, the saint has many more experiences of receiving forgiveness than the rest of us and so she knows God in a deeper way than the rest of us, and is better equipped to bring God's forgiveness and mercy to the world. We cannot imagine that we need to repent for our mere lack of awareness of God's presence, but that is only because we have spent little time in God's presence and we know little of who God is and who God calls us to be. In fact, that is the only thing for which we do have to repent, since repentance is no more than simply returning to an awareness of his presence.

We think that following Jesus is a matter of doing the things that Jesus did, and it is; but the most important thing that Jesus did was to be constantly aware of another presence besides his own. Most of us, however, go through life oblivious of God's presence, and consequently we attribute more significance to the miraculous and spectacular than to the experience of God's omnipresence in the midst of mundane life. For most of us, the idea of the manifest presence of God is an experience, while the omnipresence of God is merely theory. Jesus, however, understood the omnipresence of God, not as a theory, but as an experience. He sensed God's presence in all the events of his life and not just the spectacular and miraculous ones.

By not experiencing God's presence in the mundane, we come to think that the spectacular and miraculous represent God's presence in a way that the mundane does not. Elijah was wise enough to know that God was not simply in the spectacular and miraculous wind that split mountains and broke rocks,[10] but in the "still small voice"[11] (or as the New Revised Standard Version has it, in "a sound of sheer silence"[12]). Sadly, for many of us, we mistake the spectacular for God's presence, but God is behind the miraculous and not in it. We need to seek the God behind the miracle just as Jesus did. When Jesus performed miracles, the people were interested in the miracle, but Jesus always focused on the source of the miracle, which was God.

10. 1 Kgs 19:11.

11. 1 Kgs 19:12 KJV.

12. 1 Kgs 19:12.

Just as it is a mistake to associate God's presence with the spectacular and miraculous, so too it is a mistake to associate God's presence with the particular psychological practice or habit used to experience his presence. In developing a relationship with God, we usually develop some practice by which we experience an awareness of God's presence. Some people sense God's presence in worship, others in contemplative prayer. All too easily, however, we can come to associate God's presence exclusively with those practices, just as we can all too easily associate God's presence with the miraculous. God is always the presence we encounter through those practices, however, and God is always calling us beyond those practices. What God desires is that the awareness of his presence that we experience in worship or prayer would extend into the other areas of our lives. God's desire is that an awareness of his presence would consume the whole of our being. This is what is at the core of the gospel and it is what puts into context many of Jesus' teachings.

4

Prayer as Being in the Spirit

BOTH JESUS AND PAUL use the metaphor *flesh and spirit*. In almost all instances where that metaphor appears it seems obvious that it is good to be "in the spirit" and not good to be "in the flesh."[1] Although neither Jesus nor Paul ever explicitly tells us what it means to be in the spirit rather than in the flesh, we all too naturally suppose that *flesh* is a metaphor for the physical body. It is easy to make such an assumption since our Western culture has a long tradition of distinguishing mind from body and elevating mind or spirit while demeaning the physical body. What Paul identifies as the works of the flesh, however, include things such as idolatry, hatred, wrath, strife, sedition, and envy.[2] These are not works done by the body.

The New International Version of the Bible translates flesh (*sarx*) as "sinful nature." Of course, that is as much a metaphor as "flesh," so what is this flesh or sinful nature? The one thing it is not is that which causes God to turn away from us. Jesus tells us, in too many places to mention, that God does not turn away from us, but we turn away from God. In the parable of the banquet,[3] it is not that some are uninvited because they are not good enough to be included. Rather they chose not to attend because they have better places to be. This is the thing that I believe most charac-

---

1. Matt 26:41; Mark 14:38; John 3:6; 6:63.
2. Gal 5:19–20.
3. Matt 22:2–5.

terizes our sinful nature. It is the fact that we seek life and meaning apart from God and all that he has for us. As such, the flesh is the self that we create by seeking life and identity apart from God. That is, rather than living in the spirit, which is the self that God has created and which finds its life and meaning in God, we attempt to create meaning for ourselves by identifying with and attempting to find life in things other than God.

This does not mean that the flesh and spirit are two different selves. The spirit is simply who we are at that deeper level of who God knows us to be. It is who we are at the core of our being in our God-created self. By contrast, the flesh is the outer self that we create for ourselves as we identify with those things that become our source of meaning and purpose. The flesh is what develops when we look to the things of this world for life, meaning, and identity. It represents the trivial existence that results from focusing our attention upon all of the little gods of this world. This is our real sin, and it is what ultimately separates us from God. Our real sin is that instead of being who Jesus tells us we are, we attempt to create our own identity by attaching ourselves to the things of this world and attempting to draw life and meaning from them.

As we have seen, Jesus repeatedly tells us that God is our father[4] and we are his beloved daughters and sons,[5] and he loves us for no other reason. He does not love us because of the greatness of our charitable or pious works,[6] nor does he love our ability to keep our oaths.[7] These may be the reasons other people love us, but God is not like anyone else. In fact, the things for which other people love us are often the very things that keep us from God. Others may love us for our talent, wealth, or power. They admire such things about us, and we think they are right to do so. The things that they admire about us are what make us special, and we think they should love us because we are so special. It has taken great amounts of time and effort to acquire the talent, wealth, or power we possess, and we see such things as the virtues for which others rightfully love us. Sadly, however, we spend so much time and attention acquiring such things that

4. Matt 5:16, 45, 48; 6:1, 4, 6, 8–9, 14–15, 18, 26, 32; 7:11; 10:20, 29; 18:14, 35; Mark 11:25; Luke 6:36; 10:21; 11:13; 12:30, 32; 15:21; John 8:41; 20:17.

5. Matt 5:16, 45; 6:1, 8–9, 15; 7:1; 10:20, 29; 18:14; 23:9; Mark 11:25–26; Luke 6:36; 12:30; John 20:17.

6. Matt 6:1–4.

7. Matt 5:33–37.

we usually do not give much time or attention to God and our relationship to him. As we form an identity in the flesh by finding the source of our energy and life in the things of which Jesus warns us, we lose sight of who we are at the very core of our being. We fix our attention upon those things that give rise to the flesh, and thus we are no longer living out of the ultimate reality of who we are as God's beloved daughters and sons. This is our real sin: we have assumed a false identity.

In order to follow Jesus and live a life of prayer as he did, we have to come to live out of our identity in God rather than the identity we create for ourselves in the flesh. We need to see ourselves as God sees us, and to be "in the *spirit*" is to identify with being God's creation rather than the self we create for ourselves. Our real self, or who we are in God, is devoid of social status, prestigious occupation, power, or wealth. This self is the one that will live on in an eternity where there are no distinctions of status, prestige, power, or wealth. This is our real self, the self that will live on after the flesh or false self is long dead and forgotten. This self, and no more than this self, will spend eternity with God. One of the objectives of prayer is to return to this true self and be in the spirit rather than the flesh. The flesh never dwells in God's presence because the flesh always has its attention focused upon the worldly distractions that keep us from an awareness of God's presence. That self is never present to God and has no place in God's kingdom.

Unfortunately, we often pray in the flesh and ask God to bless the flesh and increase the distractions in our lives by adding to our wealth, power, and prestige. Sadly, many people are oblivious to their identity in God and have only an awareness of their false identity in the flesh. Some even imagine that their flesh or false identity will spend eternity in God's presence, but the Scripture tells us that the perishable cannot inherit the imperishable,[8] and our fleshly identity or false self will not be part of our eternal existence. All that we take into eternity is the life we spend in the spirit. Thus, many people will not have much to take into eternity since they spend almost all of their earthly existence in the flesh. By contrast, people who have attempted to live as Jesus lived and have spent much time in the spirit or an aware of God's presence will have a great deal of themselves to take into eternity. This idea makes even more sense when

8. 1 Cor 15:50.

we realize that our real sin or offense against God is that we live lives of distraction. Living in the flesh is a matter of being distracted by all of the things that so easily capture our attention and keep us from an awareness of God's presence.

Such a perspective gives meaning to Jesus saying that the first will be last and the last will be first, since indeed, those who had great lives in the flesh in this life will have little in the next. Likewise, those who spend much time in prayer and had little of an earthly identity will have much more of an identity in the life to come. Jesus is a beautiful example of such a life lived in the spirit to the exclusion of the flesh. He did not identify with, nor allow himself to be occupied by, those things that he warns us of in the Sermon on the Mount or throughout the rest of the Gospel. Instead, he lived a life in a constant awareness that he was God's beloved Son. He tells us to follow him and live in that same sonship. This is who we are in our spirit, and it is out of this core of our being that God wishes us to live. When we are living out of that core of our being, we are living in a state of prayer.

Sin and righteousness are essentially matters of belonging. Do we belong to God or the things of this world? Our natural tendency is to take our identity from the world. This is our sinful nature. Kingdom living occurs when we repent, and turn from those things that create the illusion that is the false self, and instead found our identity upon who we are in God. When we find ourselves beginning to identify with the world and its circumstances rather than our relationship to God, we are no longer drawing our meaning and life from God. What it means to live in the spirit rather than the flesh is to live in an awareness of who we are in relationship to God rather than who we are in relationship to the world. This is what it means to live a life in the spirit—a life of prayer.

JESUS INSTRUCTS US TO PRAY

Jesus gives instruction on how to pray; that is, how to find and dwell in our ultimate identity. He says, when you pray, "Go into your room and shut the door."[9] Of course, "go into your room and shut the door" is a metaphor that could imply several things. Augustine, in commenting about

9. Matt 6:6.

this teaching of Jesus, says that what this metaphor of going into our room and shutting the door means is that we are to go into the innermost part of our being. "We have been commanded to pray in closed chambers, by which is meant our inmost mind, for no other reason than that God does not seek to be reminded or taught by our speech in order that he may give us what we desire. He who speaks gives by articulate sounds an external sign of what he wants. But God is to be sought and prayed to in the secret place . . . which is called 'the inner man.' This he wants to be his temple."[10]

Of course, we could also understand the idea of going into our room and shutting the door in a more literal sense. When we go into our room, others no longer see us. The reason for not wanting others to see us when we pray is that when we are in the presence of others we are usually "in the flesh" rather than at the core of our being. In the presence of others, we are usually very aware of what they may think of us, and we are more concerned with our relationship with them rather than our relationship with God. By contrast, when we go into our room, or, as the King James Version says, "closet," we have the best chance to find that "inner man" of which Augustine speaks. In our closet, we have the best chance to be in our spirit rather than our flesh because in our closet there is no one there to identify us as rich, famous, talented, or however else we take pride in being identified. In our closet, we have the opportunity to assume our ultimate identity of who Jesus says we are. That is, that God is "our father" and we are his beloved daughters and sons. This is our ultimate identity, and it is by assuming that identity that we come to the proper place of prayer; that is, the place from which we can commune with God, not out of the illusion of the false self that is the flesh, but from the core of our being or who we are in the spirit.

Despite Jesus' instruction, when we generally think of prayer, we think of it as a religious activity. Religion is all about us trying to get to God, but the gospel is all about God getting to us. Likewise, religious prayer is about us communing with and getting through to God, but contemplative prayer is about God communing and getting through to us. Certainly, we have a part in that communion, but our part should focus more on being receptive and attentive to his presence rather than communicating our

10. Augustine, *De Magistro*, 70.

needs and desires, which Jesus tells us God already knows.[11] In order to become receptive, we need to be in the spirit or at the core of our being, since when we are in the flesh there are simply too many distractions that prevent us from experiencing any real sense of God's presence.

11. Matt 6:8.

5

The Practice of Prayer

MANY FINE BOOKS OFFER instruction on developing a practice of contemplative prayer, and it is not my intent to compete with them here. We should say something, however, about the practice of contemplative prayer. It is indeed a practice, and although everyone needs to find what is suitable to their particular personality and circumstance, the important thing is that we begin to practice being aware of God's presence.

The first step in beginning such a practice requires that we get out of our head. As we have mentioned, when we are living in our head, we are seldom present but are constantly being taken to thoughts of the past or future, rather than being in the present moment. There is, however, perhaps an even more important reason for getting out of our head, since when we are in our head we are in control. We like the feeling of being in control. It makes us feel secure, but such is the false security that comes from trusting the understanding through which we interpret and filter our experience. Our understanding makes sense of the world by filtering out what does not make sense and only allowing those experiences that conform to our understanding. This gives us the sense of security in that we know how things work. This is especially true of our theological understanding since it can provide a sense of eternal security. Unfortunately, it is a false sense of security since real eternal security rests in God rather than our understanding.

The other problem with finding security in our theological understanding is that it limits our God-experiences and only allows those the experience that conform to our understanding. Of course, we must filter our God-experiences, since the experience of raw data is impossible given what we now know to be our human condition. Unfortunately, however, much of modern theology was about creating an understanding so certain and precise that Christians burned one another alive when there was a lack of conformity to that understanding. Such murders were justified by claiming that the heretics were undermining God's truth, while in fact what was being undermined was the security that we seek in an understanding that purports to be certain and precise.

The reason so many people are attracted to religion is that it provides a great sense of security in that it assures us that if we simply believe the right things, or practice the right rituals and behaviors, we can be certain that God will respond the way we want him to respond. A faith in our theological understanding allows us a certain sense of control over our lives, but the faith of which Jesus speaks is about the experience of God getting hold of us. What most often prevents that experience of God getting a hold of us is our theological understanding. Theology may give us a sense of security but it does not give us the experience of God's presence. We experience God's presence when we are no longer in our heads and no longer filtering our experiences with our understanding. It is as close as we can come to pure experience, which is neither recorded nor interpreted. Jesus says, "Follow me"[1] and calls us out of our understanding and into a faith journey whereby we become ever more aware of God's presence.

LIMINAL SPACE

The mystic experience of God's presence often times occurs unintentionally in what we might call liminal space. Being in a state of liminality (from the Latin, meaning "threshold") is the experience of being on a threshold or in a state between different existential planes. Our experience of liminality may occur when our old understanding breaks down and for a time our experience of the world may be without explanation. With most of our experiences, the understanding passed on to us by our culture and

1. Matt 4:19; 8:22; 9:9; 16:24; 19:21; Mark 2:14; 8:34; 10:21; Luke 5:27; 9:23, 59; 18:22; John 1:43; 10:27; 12:26; 13:36; 21:19.

language community is sufficient to explain those experiences. At times, however, something comes into our lives that cause that understanding to break down. It could be the death of a loved one or some other traumatic event that our understanding is unable to process or interpret. At such moments without a sufficient understanding, we are no longer in our heads but are present in a way that we seldom are when our understanding is intact.

When our understanding is intact, we experience life as a routine without much consciousness of what is actually before us. Because our understanding makes life routine and predictable, we are free to be somewhere else in our minds. We are free to think about the past or the future rather than being present. When some traumatic event enters our lives, it disrupts our understanding and all of our consciousness focuses on the here and now. One circumstance has all of our attention, and we are in the liminal space of pure experience. The traumatic nature of the experience makes it impossible for our understanding to filter out the experience, but it is an experience without interpretation because the filters that normally mold and make sense of our experience are inadequate.

For many people the born-again experience came out of such liminal space. Their old understanding worked well until something happened to upset that understanding. That experience, however, opened them to the possibility of a new understanding. A few years ago, a student at my college was battling terminal cancer. She would leave for a semester to receive chemotherapy and then return in an attempt to complete her degree only to have to take the next semester off again. She was living in liminal space. The understanding that worked for the rest of us to explain our circumstances did not work for her, but because the old explanations did not work, she was open to forming a new understanding that the rest of us did not have access to because our understanding was intact. When our understanding is intact and trusted, only so much God-experience can get through. Our understanding filters out whatever does not fit with that understanding. That is how magicians do what they do. They know that our understanding will only allow us to take in so much of the experience and it will filter out those things that do not conform to our understanding, so they know we are blind to the things they are doing behind the back of our understanding. In the case of traumatic events, however, instead of filtering out the rare experience, the understanding is overwhelmed.

Such events are so powerful that we cannot ignore them in spite of their non-conformity to our understanding. Such events destabilize our understanding and we find ourselves open to experiences that our understanding might otherwise filter out. Many times, our first real God-experience comes through such an event that brings us into a liminal space where our understanding is no longer able to filter out a God-experience.

Unfortunately, after such an experience, we often come to associate the God-experience with the event, and we form a new understanding around that experience. Once again, our understanding is in charge and stands to prevent any further God-experiences unless they perfectly conform to our new understanding. Thus, in order for God to get through to us, we need future liminal experiences that destabilize our understanding. There is, however, another option. We can choose to suspend our understanding in states of contemplative prayer.

In contemplative prayer, we get out of our head, give our understanding a rest, and are simply present to God. We make a way to experience God by relaxing the filters that insist that our God-experiences conform to the words and ideas that make up our understanding. With contemplative prayer, we seek to get beyond our thinking and escape the control it has over us. That is not easily accomplished. Our minds are the great obstacle to contemplative prayer and the idea of being present. Not only does our mind insist upon leading us into thoughts of the past or future, but it also insists upon interpreting every experience, and those that do not fit with our understanding and defy interpretation the mind simply rejects. Thus, we need to get out of our head and be present to God in a way that is deeper than our understanding. We do that by refusing to let our thoughts and understanding control us. We simply need to let them go and not take them seriously. It is simply a matter of neither retaining nor resisting any ideas or attempts at interpreting what is passing through our consciousness. Simply let them pass like boats on a river until there are no boats left and only pure, uncluttered consciousness remains.

Some practitioners of contemplative prayer use a mantra in order to eliminate the ideas and understanding that keeps us in our head and constantly distract us from being present to God. Lawrence Freeman, who now heads up the *World Community of Christian Meditation* (an organization founded by John Main [1926–82]), advises using a mantra in order to eliminate distracting thoughts. A mantra is simple a word or phrase that continues to focus us and prevents the distracting thoughts from taking control of our awareness. The mantra I have used when I am being particularly distracted from being present is simply, "Jesus." By silently repeating that word, I prevent other thoughts from taking hold of me and taking me away from an awareness of God's presence. At other times, I am able to maintain an awareness of God's omnipresence without a mantra by simply refusing to allow my mind to take me into the distractions it constantly presents before me. As the distractions appear, I just repent or turn away from them and back to focus upon God's omnipresence.

Like an exercise routine, a practice of contemplative prayer is not easily established. It takes a commitment at first, but like exercise, after a while you will develop a deep love for the practice. Indeed, it will become your favorite thing and you will want to retreat into prayer constantly. That, however, is not the end of contemplative prayer. The purpose of prayer is that, once established, and having learned to access God's omnipresence, you are able to take that prayerful stance into other areas of your life. Eventually, your entire life becomes prayer, or that at least is the goal.

As we have said, Jesus' entire life was a prayer, and a large part of what it means to follow him involves making our lives states of prayer as well. God's ultimate desire is that prayer would not be a rare occasion but a way of life, and that we would become consumed by an awareness of God's presence just as Jesus was. Of course, we are constantly distracted from an awareness of his presence by just about anything, and for that reason, prayer requires a certain disciple or practice. In fact, that is exactly how Brother Lawrence (1614–91) describes prayer in his famous little book, *The Practice of the Presence of God.* He says, "I keep myself in His presence by simple attentiveness and a loving gaze upon God which I can call the actual presence of God or to put it more clearly, an habitual, silent and secret conversation of the soul with God."[2]

As we have said, God's desire is that we would be present to him as he is present to us. This awareness of God's omnipresence is the ultimate communion that is a life of prayer. Prayer may begin as a special time of being alone and still before God in order that we might experience his presence, but eventually an awareness of God's presence should consume us, and bring us into a life of prayer.

2. Brother Lawrence, *Practice,* 55.

Many years ago, I was going through a particularly difficult period, and I felt God encouraging me to spend time with him. That was not an easy thing to do since my major problem was not having enough time to accomplish all that was on my plate. I thought, if I spent more time with God, it would just make my situation worse. In spite of what I thought, however, I did manage to set Saturday afternoons apart to spend time with God. At the time, I had never read anything about contemplative or centering prayer, but I felt that this time with God should not be about reading the Bible or praying in the conventional sense. I simply got alone with God.

I am sure that those Saturday afternoons must have looked to religious people as if I was doing nothing. In fact, I was doing nothing. Nor did I receive any extraordinary revelation. There was nothing supernatural about it at all. Often I would even fall asleep, which I came to refer to as "taking a nap in the Lord." I brought nothing to that time but the belief that I was entering into God presence, and I received nothing from that time but a deep sense that God was easily accessible, and any time I wanted to be with him, he always wanted to be with me. After several months, Saturday afternoon had become my favorite time of the week.

Much to my surprise, it was at that time that I felt a prompting to give up my Saturday afternoons with God. That time had become special to me and I didn't understand why I should give it up. What I eventually came to understand was not that God wanted me to give up that special time of prayer but that I should extend that practice of his presence into all the areas of my life. God wanted Saturday afternoon to extend into Monday morning and Thursday evening.

What God desires is that we would learn to be attentive to his presence, even amid the myriad of ideas and stimuli that stream endlessly through our consciousness. What God ultimately calls us to is a life of prayer; that is, that we would be able to live in an awareness of his omnipresence and maintain a state of prayer amid all of the circumstances of our lives, just as Jesus so beautifully modeled. Of course, we constantly fall short of achieving such a life. Our hearts are prone to wander, but that fact has the interesting consequence of forcing us to live in an almost constant state of repentance. Since we so easily wander, repentance or turning back to God and an awareness of his presence is something we should find ourselves doing hundreds of times a day. As we do, we equally become aware of his forgiveness and mercy in ways that those that do not strive to live lives of prayer do not.

The great contemplative saints constantly speak of the mercy of God, and I often wondered why people who live their entire lives in prayer would so frequently speak of mercy. In time, I came to realize that it was because they were more aware than the rest of us of just how easily they were distracted from prayer or an awareness of God's presence. As we will see throughout this text, the saint realizes how easily they are distracted from an awareness of God's presence. Because of this, they are much more repentant than the rest of us and equally much more aware of God's forgiveness and mercy than the rest of us. Consequently, the saint becomes holy and more like God in terms of forgiveness because they are more aware than the rest of us of having received much forgiveness and mercy.

The gospel is all about seeing our great need for forgiveness in order that we might become forgiving by having received much forgiveness. Sadly, much of what we call prayer is not a matter of constantly returning to an awareness of God's presence in repentance and experiencing his forgiveness, but rather about thanking God for having made us righteous. Jesus tells a parable about this very point. He says,

> Two men went up to the temple to pray, one a Pharisee and the other a tax collector. The Pharisee, standing by himself, was praying thus, "God, I thank you that I am not like other people: thieves, rogues, adulterers, or even like this tax collector. I fast twice a week; I give a tenth of all my income." But the tax collector, standing far off, would not even look up to heaven, but was beating his breast and saying, "God be merciful to me, a sinner!" I tell you this man went down to his home justified rather than the other; for who exalt themselves will be humbled, but all who humble themselves will be exalted.[3]

The Pharisee in the parable thanks God that he is a good religious person, but his good religious behavior turns out not to have been good at all. He imagines that his righteousness has made him special or favored by God. Jesus, however, tells us that the sinner who cries out to God for mercy is the justified one. That is because he sees who he truly is, while the Pharisee deceives himself by his outward behavior and closes himself to the experience of God's forgiveness. By contrast, the sinner's contrite

3. Luke 18:10–14.

repentance opens him to the experience of God's forgiveness, which is the ultimate purpose of the experience of God's presence that is prayer.

What the Pharisees of Jesus' day did not understand is that the only true blessing and reason for thanksgiving is not that we are good religious people who fast and tithe, but that we have unlimited access to God's forgiveness and mercy. The only thing we can be sure of being good and for which we should be thankful is God's forgiveness and mercy. Many things that our culture considers blessings simply aggrandize the flesh and therefore we must take them in carefully measured portions, if we take them in at all. We can consume forgiveness, however, without reservation. It is the *summa bonum* and there is no vice in receiving it in excess.

6

Prayer, Forgiveness, and the Nature of Sin

WHAT IS SO STRIKING about the gospel is how obvious it makes our need for forgiveness. The standard that Jesus sets forth for righteousness should convince everyone that none of us is righteous and we all are in need of forgiveness. By contrast, if we avoid the gospel, we can convince ourselves that we are righteous. We do live by the Ten Commandments and have not committed murder or adultery. We can see ourselves as good people, until we take seriously the Jesus revelation. What Jesus reveals is that our sin is much deeper than we imagine, and we are in need of more forgiveness than we would like to imagine. That does not appear to be good news, but hidden in what appears to be bad news is the good news that God's forgiveness and mercy is greater than our sin.

God makes us in his image and likeness.[1] At birth, we bear the image of God, but it requires a lifetime to take on his likeness, especially regarding forgiveness. God desires that we would become like him in terms of forgiveness, but that only happens by our having become aware of receiving much forgiveness. Thus, in order to make us forgiving creatures after his likeness, God made us with hearts prone to wander, but along with that comes a great potential for repentance and the experience of God's

---

1. Gen 1:26.

forgiveness. We are a race of prodigals who have the potential to receive much forgiveness and therein become forgiving.

In spite of all of our efforts to invent theologies that make us feel righteous before God, the truth is that we are all prodigals in need of returning to our Father's presence through his forgiveness. Contrary to the religious notion that God wants us to be the sinless objects of his love, Jesus teaches just the opposite. The intention of the gospel is not to make us into sinless objects of God's love, but rather agents of God's forgiveness. In the verse that immediately follows what has become known as the Lord's Prayer,[2] Jesus says, "If you forgive others their trespasses, your heavenly Father will also forgive you; but if you do not forgive others, neither will your Father forgive your trespasses."[3]

The Lord's Prayer conveniently ends with verse 13 and does not include verses 14 and 15, quoted here. Likewise, we do not hear much teaching about these verses. They do not fit into our theology, so we choose to ignore them, but Jesus' words here are very pointed. We must forgive others, for if we do not forgive others, even if God would admit us to our future heavenly state, it would not be heavenly. Indeed, unless we become forgiving creatures, we will not be very happy spending eternity with a forgiving God and all of those people who God has undeservedly forgiven, but we think we have good reason to hate. Heaven will not be heavenly if we have to share it with those we hate. This is why transformation into his likeness is so important. We have to change in order to become fit for heaven, but it is not that we have to become less sinful; it is rather that we have to become forgiving.

Spending eternity with a forgiving God will be very different from what many of us would like to imagine. We like to imagine that heaven will be a place where we will realize all of our desires. What we desire, however, usually has something to do with gratifying the flesh, but God's interest is the far more profound desire is to make us into the likeness of Jesus. Being like Jesus is not about becoming sinless. Jesus never tried to provide a model for us to be sinless. In fact, the good religious people of Jesus' day saw him as a sinner. He seemed to break the stricter interpretations of the Jewish law deliberately, which the religious leaders thought they rightly understood. He did not abstain from drinking and associating

2. Matt 6:9–13.

3. Matt 6:14–15.

with disreputable people. Almost every miracle the Gospels record, Jesus did on the Sabbath, which was a great offense to many of the religious people of his day. Overall, he did not appear to be interested in creating an image of sinlessness. Instead, Jesus manifests the holiness of God through his forgiveness of the very ones who tortured and put him to death.[4] He calls us to follow him in that forgiveness in order that we might love those who do harm to us. This transformation into his forgiving likeness is what it means to be holy as he is holy.

Of course, our capacity for such forgiveness is very limited. The cliché, "To err is human, to forgive divine" may not be a cliché at all, but a profound truism. When we are offended, we desire that the offending party pay for the offense. The idea of suffering an offense for the sake of restoring the possibility of a love-relationship with the person who offended us is certainly unappealing. If the offense is serious enough, the last thing we desire is to restore relationship with them, especially if we will have to suffer something in order to accomplish that restoration. To suffer an offense for the sake of restoring relationship, however, is what forgiveness essentially is, and it is precisely this revelation of divine forgiveness that Jesus reveals to us from the cross.

I remember a story about a gang of soldiers who raped a woman and killed her entire family. Years later, while working as a nurse, a soldier was brought to her hospital on the brink of death. The nurse recognized him as the officer in charge of the men who raped her and killed her family. After eight days, the woman nursed the man back to health. Upon regaining consciousness, the doctors told him that he was only alive because of the loving care of this nurse. Upon recognizing her, he asked why she would do such a thing. She replied by telling him that she followed one who said, "Love your enemies."[5]

Now in spite of how grand her act of love and forgiveness seems, it does not approach the love and forgiveness of God. In order for it to replicate God's love and forgiveness, the nurse would have to be willing to marry the soldier and take him as her beloved just as Jesus from the cross asks his father to forgive his torturers so they might share eternity with him.[6]

4. Luke 23:34.
5. Matt 5:44.
6. Luke 23:34.

Although we marvel at such forgiveness in Jesus or anyone else who can replicate it in whatever small measure, it is not something we wish for ourselves. We much prefer to follow Jesus by being good rather than by being forgiving. The idea of the innocent suffering the offense without retaliation, for the sake of restoration, is unappealing to say the least. Given our human nature, true forgiveness of anything more than a trivial offense may be beyond what is possible. We are seriously limited in terms of forgiveness, but as limited as our capacity for forgiveness may be, it does increase with prayer. That is because true prayer, like true forgiveness, is a matter of getting out of our flesh and getting into who we are in the spirit; that is, who we are as God's beloved daughters and sons.

The flesh is what holds most of our hurts and consequently makes forgiveness so difficult. As we have seen, the flesh is the false self that we create for ourselves in our attempt to find meaning and purpose by increasing our wealth, power, or prestige. When we live exclusively in the flesh, any threat to our wealth, power, or prestige is a threat to who we are. People who live exclusively in the flesh experience every offense as a great offense. The flesh is incredibly fragile and we can very easily lose the wealth, power, or prestige upon which it rests. Thus, people who live exclusively in the flesh must meet and defeat every threat because the basis upon which the fleshly identity rests is so fragile and can be lost so easily. I recently heard a very famous billionaire say that one of his life principles was always to get even and not let any offense go unpunished. If we live in the flesh that certainly makes sense. If all we have is a fleshly identity founded upon our earthly treasure,[7] our good name and reputation,[8] or any of the other things Jesus warns us of throughout the Gospels, any threat to such things is a threat to our very being. If, however, we discover and choose to live out of that deeper self—that self that we are in our relationship with God—offenses against our flesh have little meaning because our flesh has little meaning. It is for this reason that Jesus tells us that we must be like little children.[9] We must return to that core of our being—that core of who we were in God before we created for ourselves the fleshly identity that we hold so dear.

7. Matt 6:19–21.

8. Matt 6:1–4.

9. Matt 18:3.

The way we return to such an identity in God is through prayer. The more time we spend in prayer, that is, in the spirit, the less substantial our flesh becomes and the less we take it seriously. When we spend time in the spirit as no more than God's beloved daughters or sons, it is very difficult to take offenses against our flesh seriously. Being in God's presence convinces us that we are his beloved and nothing can separate us from his love. When we are convinced of that, it is very hard to consider someone damaging our reputation, stealing our earthly possessions, or abusing us with their power as a great offense. It all pales by comparison to the experience of God's presence and the assurance that we are his beloved.

Although most of the hurts that cause us to hold unforgiveness toward others are offenses against our flesh or the identity we have created for ourselves apart from God, some offenses are deep wounds and not merely flesh wounds. Things like childhood sexual abuse or other forms of trauma in childhood may have occurred before we had the chance to develop a flesh. Such deep wounds may require more in the way of forgiveness than simply letting go of the flesh. Even in such cases, however, the solution is a forgiveness that requires that we return to that deeper self of who we are in God. Deep wounds, like flesh wounds, still require forgiveness, and real forgiveness only happens out of the core of our being when we assume our ultimate identity as God's beloved daughters and sons. Once we can achieve an awareness of God as our father and the fact that nothing can separate us from his love, releasing the hurts of this life through forgiveness becomes a real possibility. It is only from the security of knowing who we are in God at the core of our being that we can experience the letting go that real forgiveness entails, and the only way to that core of our being is prayer.

If we are to be like Jesus and forgive as he forgives, we must live a life of prayer—a life of being present to God from the core of our being. As long as we are in the flesh, the best we can do is to make a pretense to forgiveness. Forgiveness in the flesh is simply a work of the flesh. It puffs us up and makes us into religious people with more reason to be proud of our flesh. Jesus constantly attacked the Pharisees of his day for this very reason. The Pharisees were what we would consider *good* people. They kept the Jewish law probably better than any group of Jews ever had, but they thought that their behavior made them righteous. In particular, they thought that if they avoided certain sinful behaviors they would be pleasing to God. Jesus does not condemn them for their behavior, but because they were proud of the religious, false self, which they had created and believed was pleasing to God.

Jesus knew that sin (i.e., our offense against God) occurs long before we commit some destructive act like adultery or murder. Although our culture may equate sin with such moral evils and righteousness with the avoidance of such evils, our offense against God occurs when we pursue fleshly identities, rather than an identity in God. Rather than desiring to be present and attentive to God, we choose to focus our attention upon the things of this world. Remember the only thing a lover really desires from their beloved is their attention or presence. I know a pastor who says, "My wife likes my presence more than my presents."

Recall again the parable of the banquet,[10] where Jesus tells us that the people who do not come to the banquet are not at a bordello or crack house but they are doing business and getting married. We think that there is nothing evil about doing business or getting married, but it is what the people in the parable choose rather than being at the banquet, and we constantly choose to be somewhere else rather than at the banquet God has prepared for us. Our sin is that we choose to be almost anywhere rather than in God's presence. This is our sin or the offense God suffers when we simply turn away from him and seek a life apart from his presence, and all that comes from the experience of his presence. What God suffers is the broken heart of a father who desires so much more for his daughters and sons than the lives they continually choose for themselves. What grieves God is the fact that we seek meaningless, trivial lives apart from an awareness of his presence and provision.

Because Jesus understood God as *our* Father[11] in a way like no one else, he also understood the nature of sin like no one else. What Jesus understood was that our real sin or offense against God is that we leave his presence and go off like the Prodigal Son to find a life for ourselves apart from our Father.[12] Thus, God's heart is broken long before our behavior brings evil and destruction into the world. This is the radical nature of sin, which we find in the Gospels. The word *radical* comes from the Latin,

10. Luke 14:16–20.

11. Matt 5:16, 45, 48; 6:1–18; 7:11, 20; 10:29; 18:14; 23:9; Mark 11:25; Luke. 6:36; 12:30; John 20:17.

12. Luke 15:11–32.

radix—meaning root, and that is exactly what Jesus is revealing. He is showing us that our sin is rooted in our turning away from God. When Jesus speaks of sin, he is always addressing it at this level. Since we generally only understand sin as it develops into some form of destructive behavior, we miss a lot of the Jesus revelation.

Because we misunderstand sin, we also misunderstand other things as well. One thing that we especially misunderstand because of our wrong concept of sin is the idea of repentance. Since our culture understands that our sins are the terrible evils we have done to one another, we imagine that great remorse is required in order to receive forgiveness. We think that we should only forgive when there is great remorse, and if someone is not sorry for what they have done, we would be foolish to forgive them. This, however, is very different from the picture Jesus paints of both forgiveness and repentance.

In the story that Jesus tells of the Prodigal Son,[13] the prodigal does admit to having sinned but there does not seem to be any deep remorse on his part, and he returns to his father because he is hungry. More importantly, the father of the prodigal does not look for any remorse within his son. Neither is the father interested in making his son understand the grief he has caused him. Unlike ourselves, who insist that those we forgive come to us with remorse and understand the extent of the offense, the father of the prodigal is only interested in his son's return. There is no hint that the father's forgiveness requires that remorse accompany his son's return. Unlike most of us, who might have mixed feelings over the fact that although our son has returned, he has squandered half of our estate, there is no room in the father's heart for anything but joy. This is the way Jesus understood both God's forgiveness and our repentance. The nature of God's forgiveness is such that it requires nothing from us but a turning back to God from whatever has distracted us and taken us from his presence.

We see the same kind of forgiveness with Jesus and the criminal crucified along with him. There is no indication of great remorse on the criminal's part. He simply turns to Jesus, and asks Jesus to remember him. Jesus responds by saying, "Truly I tell you, today you will be with me in paradise."[14] It seems that Jesus' view of sin and repentance is very differ-

13. Luke 15:11–32.
14. Luke 23:43.

53

ent from our cultural view, and although we call ourselves Christians and claim to be followers of Christ, we adhere to our cultural view of sin and repentance rather than what Jesus sets forth in the Gospels. Our culture tells us that sin only exists when it is external and involves destructive behavior. True, our destructive behavior is the result of sin, and it is certainly something we should avoid, but Jesus is always addressing the root of the sin and not how it manifests itself in destructive behavior.

One of the reasons we have such trouble understanding Jesus and the Gospels is because things are so different with human beings than they are with God. We judge a person's behavior and equate it with sin or righteousness because we are unable to judge the hearts of others the way that God is able. Our judicial system punishes bad behavior, not wayward thoughts, but we grieve the heart of God long before any destructive behavior appears. We may think that as long as we stop short of an evil act, we have done no harm; but the attitude of our heart and the focus of our mind are what truly establish who we are. This is God's ultimately concern. What makes us immoral in society's eyes is that we commit murder or adultery, but God loves the murderer and adulterer and knows that the evil and destruction they have done is not simply to another but to themselves. Furthermore, that destruction comes to them long before they actually commit murder or adultery. The destruction begins when their hearts and minds become preoccupied with anger or lust rather than God.

God has made us to be creatures that eternally dwell in his presence. This is our ultimate nature—it is who we are at our core. Sin is the perversion of that nature. It occurs every time we depart from an awareness of God's presence and focus our attention on things other than God and the things he has for us. This being the nature of sin, the solution is simply to turn back to God, who is always willing to forgive with rejoicing and celebration over our return. To see sorrow and remorse as a necessary part of repentance is to make our relationship with God based upon something other than God's forgiveness and mercy.

Although remorse may often accompany our repentance, it is not required and has no effect upon God's forgiveness. If it did, we would all be in trouble since we are usually oblivious of our real sin and therefore feel no remorse over it. As we have seen, our real sin, which grieves the heart of God, is our failure to give God the attention that a love-relationship requires. Our sin is that we do not love God with our whole heart, soul, mind, and strength. This great commandment, which none of us keep, should be the source of our remorse, but it is something that only a few contemplative saints have understood.

Of course, this does not mean that we should not have remorse over our sin. As we become more aware of our sin, we do experience remorse over it. As we realize how far short we have fallen from the life God has for us, and how we grieve the heart of God as we choose so much less than the fullness of life he had for us in Christ Jesus, remorse does have a place. It is not, however, an essential place, and, as we have said, it has no effect upon the heart of God.

Although remorse is not ultimately necessary, and has no effect upon God's forgiveness, what is necessary is that we become aware of God's forgiveness. God can extend forgiveness to us, but we become forgiving people only as we become aware of being the constant recipients of God's forgiveness. To that end, we need to become more aware of our sin, since the more aware we are of our sin, the more we are aware of God's forgiveness.

7

The Sermon on the Mount
and the Presence of God

WE TEND TO SHY away from the Sermon on the Mount.[1] We do not know what to make of it, since it goes so much against our cultural prejudice concerning the nature of sin. Our culture tells us that sins are moral evils that somehow offend God. We even find Scriptures throughout the Bible to support that cultural concept. What Jesus sets forth in the Sermon on the Mount, however, does not look like what we take to be moral evils, yet Jesus equates them with sin and warns us of them. Jesus obviously has a concept of sin that is very different from what we conceive of as sin. So, what is it about the things that Jesus mentions in the Sermon on the Mount that makes them sins? If sin is an offense against God, what is it that is so offensive about oaths, worry, earthly treasure, anger, or even lust, which we reason do not overtly hurt anyone since they do not necessarily involve our behavior? I am convinced that Jesus identifies such things as sin because they are the very things that take us out of a state of prayer. They are the things that we choose to focus our attention and awareness upon rather than God.

As we have said, Jesus was constantly aware of his Father's presence. His entire life was a prayer, and he calls us to live as he lived in a similar state of prayer. From that perspective, the Sermon on the Mount is all

1. Matt 5:1—7:29.

about teaching us to pray. What we call the Lord's Prayer may be at the center of the Sermon on the Mount,[2] but what comes both before and after it is also instruction concerning prayer; that is, Jesus instructs us on how to be present and attentive to God. He does so by warning us of those things that so easily take us from an awareness of God's presence.

Contrary to what many people think, sin does not cause God to turn away from us but rather sin is our turning away from him as we fix our attention upon, and become preoccupied with, those things of which Jesus warns us throughout the Sermon on the Mount. They are our sins and the things that keep us from an awareness of God presence or a state of prayer.

Consider what he says: He tells us that we are not to make oaths,[3] we are not to seek retribution,[4] we are to love our enemies,[5] and when we give alms, pray, or fast, we are to do it in a way not to have anyone notice.[6] He also tells us that we are not to worry, seek earthly treasure, or make judgments concerning others.[7] What a strange set of dictates. They seem to be very different from the kind of behavioral prescriptions we usually associate with moral dictates.

What they do seem to be, however, are those things that typically capture our attention and keep us from an awareness of God's presence. They are the things that human beings typically seek to draw life from rather than God. What Jesus is warning us of are all the false sources of identity—the things that give meaning and motivation to so many, but in the end are disappointing sources of life. Our real sin, and what separates us from God, is that we seek life and meaning apart from God; that is, God is not in all of our thoughts. Rather, our time and attention are given to the gods of this world, which we worship and attempt to draw life and meaning from.

What Jesus is addressing in the Sermon on the Mount are those things that cause us to turn away from God. The first thing he warns us of is anger. The act of murder does not separate us from God. We separate ourselves from God, and the life he has for us, long before we commit an

2. Matt 6:9–13.
3. Matt 5:27–28.
4. Matt 5:27–28.
5. Matt 5:43–44.
6. Matt 6:1–18.
7. Matt 6:19—7:2.

act of murder. We sin, and separate ourselves from God, when the source of our energy—the thing that motivates us—becomes anger rather than God. "You have heard that it was said to the people long ago, 'Do not murder, and anyone who murders will be subject to judgment.' But I tell you that anyone who is angry with his brother will be subject to judgment."[8]

For many of us, our anger is our god and the source of our energy and life. It is what motivates us. Athletes and other competitors often find strength and motivation in anger, but Jesus tells us God is to be our source of strength. Likewise, Jesus says, "You have heard that it was said, 'Do not commit adultery.' But I tell you that anyone who looks at a woman lustfully has already committed adultery with her in his heart."[9]

Our contemporary culture sees nothing wrong with imagined infidelity, but Jesus tells us that our sin lies in the lust and not simply in the realization of the infidelity. That is because we remove ourselves from God's presence, not when we engage in forbidden sex, but when we think about it. It is the lust or thought of sex that consumes our attention and turns out focus away from God. It is not the act of adultery that so displeases God that he turns away from us, but rather that we turn away from him when we fix our attention upon the things after which we lust.

The third thing that Jesus mentions in the Sermon on the Mount is that we are not to make oaths. Moses had given prohibitions against the breaking of oaths that we have sworn,[10] but now Jesus tells us we should make no oaths at all. "You have heard that it was said to the people long ago, 'Do not break your oath, but keep the oaths you have made to the Lord.' But I tell you, Do not swear at all . . . for you cannot make even one hair white or black."[11]

First-century Christians saw pledging allegiance to anything other than God as a sin. The early Christian martyrs died not because they were Christians but because of their refusal to swear allegiance to pagan gods. You could be a Christian in the Roman Empire, but you had to pledge alliance to the Roman gods as well. It was *this* that the early Christians refused to do and they paid for it with their lives. The early Christians would never have pledged allegiance to the flag of the United States, because they

8. Matt 5:21–22.

9. Matt 5:27–28.

10. Deut 7:8; Num 30:2.

11. Matt 5:33–36.

took Jesus teachings seriously. Christians today are quite different. We pay little attention to Jesus' teachings and focus almost exclusively upon the last three hours of Jesus' life. We want him to be our Savior but not our Teacher and Master. We ignore Jesus and side with our culture, which tells us that it is noble to keep our word and promises even when those oaths cause us to end up on the side of evil. Of course, breaking our oaths is a problem as well. Thus, Jesus tells us to promise our commitment to no one or no thing but God.

The real problem with swearing oaths is that it, like anger and lust, is something we are quick to identify with and use as a source of energy and motivation. We boast to others and take pride in giving our word, as if there was power in our words and their ability to control circumstances. Jesus tells us that we are not in control over the circumstances of our lives and thus to swear to do this or that is a false witness and a boast in a power we do not have. We would like to think that we are men or women of our word and, once given, our word is enough to motivate us to do what we have sworn. If we are honest with ourselves, we see what a lie that is and how powerless our sworn oaths are. Jesus reminds us of that powerlessness and that we cannot make one hair white or black.[12] We, however, love the illusion of power within ourselves and therefore swear oaths, as if we were able to will to do this or that. God's desire is that we would draw our power from an awareness and identification with his presence.

Jesus next addresses our idea of retribution. "You have heard that it was said, 'Eye for eye, and tooth for tooth.' However, I tell you, Do not resist an evil person. If someone strikes you on the right cheek turn to him the other also."[13]

The Mosaic Law had allowed for retribution, but it seems that it, like divorce, was hardly God's ultimate standard. Ultimately, retribution is a source of sin or separation from God, since it can easily possess us and cause us to look to it rather than God for peace and satisfaction when we are injured. Jesus warns us against such a false source of hope. Solace is to be found in God alone.

Additionally, retribution, and the idea of justice it fuels, also gives us a false sense of righteousness that keeps us from repentance and the experience of God's mercy. Our sense of justice and the punishing of evil-

12. Matt 5:36.
13. Matt 5:38–39.

doers make us feel that it is someone else that is in need of forgiveness and mercy, and not us.

The next thing Jesus tells us probably goes farther beyond what Moses had given in the law than anything else Jesus ever said. The people of the Old Testament were in no way ready to receive this commandment, just as most of us are still not ready to receive it today. Jesus says, "You have heard that it was said, 'Love your neighbor and hate your enemies.' But I tell you: Love your enemies and pray for those who persecute you that you may be sons of your Father in heaven."[14]

This is not merely a difficult commandment; it is an *a priori* impossibility. Enemies are by definition people we do not love. If we love our enemies, the idea of an "enemy" loses its meaning. Perhaps Jesus could ask us not to take revenge upon our enemies or maybe even not to hate them, but to love them seems beyond the realm of human possibility. That, however, may be just the point. Indeed, the only way it is humanly possible is if God is the source of our identity and we connect with him from the core of our being, just as Jesus had. Of course, everything Jesus says in the Sermon on the Mount is intent upon making just that point.

Following the command to love our enemies, Jesus then begins to command us concerning religious activities. When we give to the needy, we should do it in a way that we do not gain recognition from other human beings. Thus, it is not enough that we give, but we must give with the right attitude and that right attitude is that we give without a desire for recognition.[15] This may seem strange since previously Jesus said, "Let your light shine before men, that they might see your good deeds and praise your father in heaven."[16] Obviously, if we give with the intent of others seeing our good deeds, it is not a good deed; it is intent upon bringing glory to our flesh or false self. Charity for the sake of recognition makes prestige and reputation the source of our motivation. What should motivate us is that we have begun to take on the heart of God because we have become aware of an identity ultimately founded in God.

There is a similar situation with the religious practices of prayer and fasting. Like almsgiving, we are to do it in a way that no one but God knows. It is not enough that we pray and fast, but we must do it with-

14. Matt 5:43–44.
15. Matt 6:1.
16. Matt 5:16.

out reputation or esteem being our motivation. It is a sin when we do it for reputation or esteem, since it causes us to focus our awareness upon other people and thoughts of their reaction to us, rather than upon God. Remember, sin is all about our attention being somewhere else rather than fixed upon God. The fact that we are God's beloved daughters and sons is our only source of worth—everything else is an illusion, which Jesus is trying to expose. There simply is no life in an existence founded upon the way other human beings identify us. To seek life apart from God is the root cause of all manner of evil, for it separates us from our only true source of worth and meaning. After we have been in his presence for ten thousand years, we will see how shallow and meaningless human fame and recognition really was, and why Jesus tried to expose this illusion. Like fame and recognition among human beings, earthly treasure has a similar deadly effect when we look to it rather than God for life. Jesus says, "Do not store up for yourselves treasures on earth, where moth and rust destroy, and where thieves break in and steal. But store up for yourselves treasures in heaven."[17]

Jesus knows how easily we attach ourselves to the things of this world and how easily they, rather than God, become the source of our identity and provide a false sense of worth. Most people, especially successful people, draw their energy from their treasure and the things they have accomplished in this life. Jesus tells us that such treasures are a fleeting source of worth and we will soon be disappointed if we put our hope in them rather than God.

Jesus next tells us not to worry. Certainly being frightened is not a sin, but as we allow what scares us to remain in our lives and become worry, we certainly do sin, since our worry is the thing that has captured our attention and keeps us from an awareness of God's presence. Anxiety is the opposite of the kind of faith to which Jesus calls us. When we are anxious about many things, our attention is not on God. With worry at the center of our being, God is not in all of our thoughts, and it is not God, but worry, that energizes and defines us. For many people, worry is at the center of their lives. It is their source of identity and occupies the place that only God should occupy.

17. Matt 6:19–20.

Finally, Jesus says, "Do not judge."[18] That, however, is what we most want to do. What is behind so much of our theology is a desire to have a standard by which we can judge the saved from the unsaved, the godly from the ungodly, and the moral from the immoral. We think we can judge what is good and what is evil, but the truth is that we form our judgments out of the insufficient understanding that is our limited perspective within time and place. God sees things from the perspective of eternity, which is very different from our perspective.

The serpent may have told Adam and Eve that if they ate the forbidden fruit they would know as God knows,[19] but that was a lie. Not everything in the Bible is true. Divine revelation can reveal lies as well, and what the serpent told Adam and Eve was certainly a lie. We lack God's eternal perspective, and therefore cannot tell the wheat from the weeds.[20] Sadly, what religion so often offers is an understanding that makes us feel that we are capable of making judgments concerning righteousness. By contrast, any serious reading of the Sermon on the Mount should convince us that Jesus' understanding of sin and righteousness is very different from our own, and therefore any judgments we make based on our understanding are going to be very different from Jesus' judgments.

Jesus' warning against judgments ends his litany on sin and righteousness. He then concludes the Sermon on the Mount by saying, "Ask and it will be given to you; seek and you will find; knock and the door will be opened to you. For everyone who asks receives; he who seeks finds; and to him who knocks, the door will be opened."[21]

In light of the impossible standard that Jesus has set forth in the Sermon on the Mount, it seems obvious that what we need to ask and seek is that God would extend mercy toward us for having failed to live by the standard that Jesus sets forth. What we need to ask is that God would give us a spirit of repentance in order that we can turn away from the false gods of this world and experience God's presence through the forgiveness that he so faithfully provides. We will always be distracted from an awareness of God's presence by the false gods and false sources of life that we constantly encounter in this world. What we need is a grace

18. Matt 7:1.
19. Gen 3:4–5.
20. Matt 13:24–30.
21. Matt 7:7–8.

that would allow us to not tire of repentance so we can continually turn away from those things that fuel the false self and turn back toward God who is the ultimate source of our identity. God is willing to provide all the forgiveness and mercy we need, all we need to do is be willing to live in a state of almost constant repentance. If we simply have to ask, then what we need to ask is that repentance would fill our soul and we would live in a constant state of turning away from all those things that so easily entrap us and keep us from drawing our strength and energy—our life and meaning—from God alone.

The good news we have received, and are to preach to the world, is that God is not calling us to obey a moral law of endless requirements. He is calling us to a relationship, and we become aware of that relationship through repentance or simply turning from the false gods that surround and engulf us. We do not need to find him, we only need to turn from those false gods and idols that capture our attention and keep us from an awareness of the God who is always there. Whenever we do that, we are in his presence. It may feel like nothing, since it is indeed no thing, but the pure presence of being that is God.

Of course, in order to turn from the things of this world, which so easily capture us and hold us in their sway, we have to see a need to do so. Most people see no problem with loving the gods of this world. They are happy with their earthy treasure and the reputation they have taken so long to acquire. They like the life that comes from their lust, anger, and even their worry. These things define them and they cannot imagine an identity apart from them. It is all that they are and they feel that without these things, they would be nothing. It is, however, in our nothingness that we find the God who is our real source of identity. This is why Jesus tells us at the beginning of the Sermon on the Mount, "Blessed are the poor in spirit."[22]

THE BEATITUDES

Jesus begins the Sermon on the Mount with what we have come to know as the Beatitudes. The Beatitudes explain who the truly blessed are. The rest of the Sermon on the Mount explains the reason they are blessed; that is, they are not as susceptible as the rest of us who draw our identity and

22. Matt 5:3.

life from the false gods of this world. Those who lack a fleshly identity in the things of this world are better able to become aware of their identity in God through their detachment.

Unfortunately, many religious people are not lacking in such a fleshly identity. They feel good about themselves and are proud of how much they have accomplished, all the good they have done, and all the evil they have avoided. If they consider what Jesus says, however, they would see that they have stored up treasures on earth, sought the approval of men, and proudly stood in their own judgments. In dire contrast to such people, Jesus tells us that the truly blessed ones are the "poor in spirit."[23] They are blessed, and theirs is the kingdom of heaven, because they have nothing but God as their source of identity and self-worth. They are free from many of the sources from which the false self draws life.

After telling us that the poor in spirit are the truly blessed ones, Jesus goes on to tell us of other things that constitute our blessedness.

> Blessed are those who mourn, for they will be comforted.
> Blessed are the meek, for they will inherit the earth.
> Blessed are those who hunger and thirst for righteousness, for
> they will be filled.
> Blessed are the merciful, for they will be shown mercy.
> Blessed are the pure in heart, for they will see God.[24]

Instead of pointing to things that most of us see as blessings, Jesus tells us that the blessed are those that mourn, are meek, hunger and thirst for righteousness, are merciful, and pure of heart. The world tells us that we are blessed if we never suffer loss and are proud and satisfied with our righteousness, but such people live unto themselves and have no need of God. The ones that know God are those that find their identity in him. They find no ultimate value in the blessings of this world and find worth in God alone. They find no righteousness in themselves and therefore they seek mercy and find it in God. These are the pure in heart, for they find life in God alone. Jesus tells us that the pure of heart will see God, and we only see God only when we are pure of heart. We lack purity of heart because of all the distraction that constantly possesses us and keep us from an awareness of the God who is ever present. We achieve purity

23. Matt 5:3.
24. Matt 5:4–8.

of heart in prayer by continually turning away from those distractions and back to an awareness of God presence.

If we accept what Jesus is setting forth as the kind of life to which God is calling us, we should realize how poor in spirit and in need of mercy we really are. In light of the standard that Jesus sets forth, we should mournfully and meekly hunger after a righteousness that is beyond us. If we accept Jesus' teachings in the Sermon on the Mount, we should be convinced of the truth of the Beatitudes, and that the only blessed ones are those poor, meek, and mournful souls that find a humble state of repentance from which to experience God's mercy.

MORALITY AND THE SERMON ON THE MOUNT

Most people do not know what to make of the Sermon on the Mount. They want religion to be all about morality, and the Sermon on the Mount is obviously not about behavior, so they ignore it. They want God to be a moral cop who rewards good behavior and punishes bad behavior. They want God to be the ultimate enforcer of a moral, social order, so we can imagine that our good behavior pleases God and other people's bad behavior displeases him. Jesus' teachings are constantly addressing this and showing us how wrong we are about what we imagine to be the basis for our relationship with God.

The only thing that pleases God is our presence, and the only thing that grieves the heart of God is our lack of presence. Our behavior may be the basis for our relationships with other human beings but God is always looking for something deeper than behavior. This should be obvious from the story of the Prodigal Son, where the father is grieved over the son's absence and delighted when the son is once again present. It is also obvious in numerous other places throughout the Gospels, but none more so than in the Sermon on the Mount. There Jesus constantly points to the fact that it is not behaviors like adultery or murder that effect our relationship with God, but internal conditions of the heart like lust, anger, judgment, and worry. Not that they offend God and cause God to turn away from us, but that they are what typically capture our attention and keep us from an awareness of God's presence. The sin is that we are distracted and not attentive, and being attentive is what it means to love God with all of our heart, soul, mind, and strength.

It is not really anger that is the sin, but a lack of awareness of God's presence, and anger is the cause of the lack of awareness. If anger itself were the sin, then Jesus seems to have sinned when he drove the moneychangers from the temple[25] with what surely appears to have been anger.[26] If anger itself were the sin, then Jesus fails to live by his own standard. Of course, that is only if we fail to understand anger as sinful because it is one of those things that capture our attention and keeps us from an awareness of God's presence. Jesus was constantly aware of his Father's presence, in a way that we seldom are. He was never distracted as we so easily are. With us, behavior that we identify as angry almost always betrays our internal state of drawing our life and energy from some source other than God. The problem with anger is that for most of us it is what easily takes our attention away from God and fixes our focus on the object of our anger. That does not seem to have been a problem for Jesus. Nothing turned his attention from the Father.

Likewise, Jesus warns us of worry,[27] upon which so many of us become fixated. Jesus, however, sweats blood in the garden before his crucifixion,[28] but when Jesus worries, it does not take him from an awareness of God's presence the way it so often does with us. Indeed, when worry draws us into God's presence it is a good thing.

Another example of Jesus' behavior not seeming to match up with what he says in the Sermon on the Mount is that he tells us not to pray in front of others, but to go into a private place where we are alone with God.[29] An entire chapter in John's Gospel, however, has Jesus praying in front of his disciples.[30] Jesus is not failing to live by his own standard, because what he is setting forth in the Sermon on the Mount is not behavior that is displeasing to God. Rather, he is warning us of all the distractions that so easily take us from an awareness of God's presence; and although we are easily distracted from an awareness of God's presence when we are in the company of others, Jesus never was. Jesus did not allow his anger,

---

25. Matt 21:12–13.
26. Matt 5:21–22.
27. Matt 6:25.
28. Luke 22:44.
29. Matt 6:5–6.
30. John 17:1–26.

worry, or public prayer to distract him, but he knew that these were the very things that do distract us.

The central theme of the gospel, and what most characterizes Jesus' life, is his constant awareness of his Father's omnipresence. A great part of his ministry teaches us to practice an awareness of that presence. Jesus knew that God is always present to us and never distracted from us the way we are constantly distracted from him. This is what the great saints also understood: that we are still in the Garden, and, like Adam, God still walks with us, but none of us lives in an awareness of the divine presence the way Jesus did. We do achieve such states of awareness, however, in prayer, and following Jesus is largely about making our lives into lives of prayer or the awareness of God's presence.

One of the most interesting things about this level of prayer, which is the simple awareness of God's presence, is that it reveals the depth of our sin as nothing else can. Only as we attempt to focus our attention upon God and be present, in the way that being in love demands, do we discover what inept lovers we are. As we have seen, we are distracted by just about anything, and when we try to really pray and focus our attention on God, we find that thirty seconds is a long time to go without being distracted by those ideas that constantly invade our consciousness. Imagine a human being who you profess to love, but were unable to give your attention for more than thirty seconds. Imagine how frustrated they would be with your attempt at loving them. Fortunately, unlike a human lover who would respond by finding someone else, God's response is always forgiveness.

The experience of prayer or the practice of God's presence should convince us that we are incapable of the great commandment to love God with our whole heart, soul, mind, and strength. The experience of that failure, however, is the very thing that leads us to the experience of his forgiveness, and the experience of his forgiveness is what is at the heart of the transformation that makes us into his likeness. As mentioned earlier, those who spend much time in deep prayer recognize their need for forgiveness more than the rest of us, since they recognize how easily their attention is diverted and how they constantly fail to give God the attention that a love relationship requires.

8

Getting at the Heart of the Gospel

MANY PEOPLE THINK THAT the born-again experience is at the heart of the gospel. Indeed, Jesus does say, "No one can see the kingdom of God without being born from above."[1] In a way, the "born from above" or born-again experience is essential in that the journey to which Jesus calls us does begin when we become aware of God's presence in our lives. That awareness does resemble a rebirth experience, before which, as Jesus says, we are not even able to see the kingdom of God.[2] Therefore, such an experience may be essential to the Christian life, but it is only a beginning and not the end or purpose of the life to which God calls us. We may begin with the "born from above" or born-again experience but the Christian life is much more about the journey upon which we embark when we decide to follow him. In contrast to Jesus saying, "You must be born again,"[3] which he says late at night, to one person, in one of the four Gospels, he says, "follow me" seventeen times throughout the four Gospels.[4] So why do people identify themselves as *born-again* Christians rather than *follow-me* Christians? The most obvious reason is that to be a

---

1. John 3:3. The New International Version says "born again" rather than the more literal "born from above."

2. John 3:5.

3. John 3:7.

4. Matt 4:19; 8:22; 9:9; 16:24; 19:21; Mark 2:14; 8:34; 10:21; Luke 5:27; 9:23, 59; 18:22; John 1:43; 10:27; 12:26; 13:36; 21:19.

"follow me" Christian demands much more from us than a simple born-again experience.

Of course, this is not to deny the born-again experience. Such an experience may be the beginning of a new life, but many take that experience to mean that they have become a new creature made in the likeness of Jesus. But the deep changes of real transformation do not come in an instant. Perhaps some external, behavioral changes do occur directly after a born-again experience, but they just mark the beginning of the journey. If we do not understand this, we all too easily believe that we already have taken on the mind of Christ, bear the likeness of Jesus, and therefore have no problem with interpreting the Jesus revelation correctly. Consequently, we create a tribal Jesus after our own likeness rather than humbly giving ourselves over to a lifelong transformation into his likeness.

It is very natural that we begin with a tribal interpretation of the gospel, since we inherit the understanding through which we create our interpretation from parents, pastors, Sunday School teachers, and television preachers. Their interpretation of the gospel often shies away from the radically divine Jesus of the Gospels and has very little to do with the things Jesus said and did. Contrary to the things that Jesus said and did, American Christianity, as practiced by the older establishment, is largely about morality—specifically family values and opposition to homosexuality and abortion. Interestingly, Jesus does not seem concerned with any of these things. He never addressed the matters of abortion or homosexuality, although they were both rampant in the Roman world of his day. Roman law allowed for infanticide as well as abortion, and sex with members of the same sex was common throughout the ancient world. Jesus does address family values, but he has nothing good to say. Instead of praising the value of family, he says, "Whoever comes to me and does not hate father and mother, wife and children, brother and sister, yes, even life itself, cannot be my disciples."[5] Or, "For I have come to set a man against his father, and a daughter against her mother, and a daughter-in-law against her mother-in-law; and ones foes will be members of one's own household."[6] Certainly, in other parts of the Bible we can find good things said about family values, as well as prohibitions against abortion and homosexuality. So, rather than following the one we claim to be God incarnate, we

5. Luke 14:26.

6. Matt 10:35.

develop a theory about the Bible being a revelation of who God ultimately and objectively is. Thus, when Jesus tells us to love our enemies,[7] we point to other places where the Scripture tells us to kill our enemies, including their women and children.[8] Rather than believing that the Scripture is a progressive revelation, which culminates with the gospel, we put our faith in a theory about Scripture being an objective revelation in order to use the rest of Scripture to negate the Jesus revelation. Consequently, we can argue that although Jesus tells us to love our enemies, in other places the Scripture tells us to kill our enemies. Sometimes God wants us to love our enemies and sometimes he wants us to kill our enemies. We usually decide that this is a time for killing rather than loving.

Within other, more charismatic strains of Christians, the emphasis is not as much on morality, but rather worship. Jesus, however, does not seem interested in being the object of worship. Indeed, Jesus never tells us to worship him and only twice is the phrase "worship me" used in the Gospels. Once is when Satan asks Jesus to worship him. He tells Jesus, "All these I will give you, if you fall down and worship me."[9] The other appearance of the phrase "worship me" occurs when Jesus quotes the prophet Isaiah: "You hypocrites! Isaiah prophesied rightly about you when he said: 'This people honors me with their lips, but their hearts are far from me; in vain do they worship me, teaching human precepts as doctrines.'"[10]

Although Jesus never tells us to worship him, it is certainly easier to worship Jesus than to follow him. This is not to say that we should not worship Jesus. Jesus is certainly worthy of worship, and if we do not worship him, we very quickly begin to worship ourselves or someone else equally unworthy of worship. Worship is part of the Christian life, but like the born-again experience, worship is not the *essential* part; in fact, worshiping Jesus can often be a way to avoid following Jesus.

Another contemporary version of the gospel is what we hear from television preachers. The vast majority of them tell us that the gospel is all about God desiring to bless us physically and financially in proportion to our faith, which we demonstrate through our giving. There is truth in this but it is hardly the central truth of the gospel.

7. Matt. 5:44; Luke 6:35.
8. Josh 6:20–21.
9. Matt 4:9; Luke 4:7.
10. Matt 15:7–9; Mark 7:6–7.

Perhaps the worst contemporary interpretation of the gospel is that of a formula whereby we see ourselves as having an inside track to God because we are special and have found a way to be righteous in his eyes. The words of Jesus, however, constantly warn the religious insiders of their need of repentance. Jesus always resists the religious establishment and extends grace to outsiders who know that they are sinners in need of mercy.

Most of these popular notions of the Christian life develop because we refuse to see the truly radical nature of the gospel. We insist upon interpreting the gospel in ways that will accommodate our cultural concepts, norms, and values; but the truth is that Jesus' words, if taken seriously, do violence to our cultural understanding. Jesus tells us that God's values are very different from our own, and that "what is prized by human beings is an abomination in the sight of God."[11] This is why the way Jesus calls us to follow is a narrow way and few find it.[12] What most of us find is a tribal Jesus, who, unlike the Jesus of the Gospels, looks like us and has concepts and values very much like our own. Our tribal notion of Jesus is the very thing that keeps us from the fullness of the gospel and the fullness of life God has for us. That is because our tribal notion of Jesus keeps us from the journey of following Jesus into a deeper and more radical notion of who God is and who we are in relationship to God. It assures us that we already know Jesus, and he is very much like us. Therefore, there is no need for a journey into a deeper understanding.

The Jesus of the Gospels is very different from the tribal Jesus who has our values and wants us to realize those values by improving our moral behavior. What we have argued throughout this text is that what it means to follow Jesus and live as he lived is not about living lives of sinless moral behavior, but rather about living as he lived in a constant state of prayer or an awareness of God's presence. That does not immediately sound like good news. In fact, it sounds like bad news in that none of us lives such a life. It is good news, however, since it is our failure to live as Jesus lived that leads us into repentance, and the experience of God's forgiveness and mercy, which in time makes us into his forgiving and merciful likeness. This is what is so radical about the gospel. It is the fact that we come to God, as we have repeatedly said, not by doing it right, but by doing it

11. Luke 16:15.

12. Matt. 7:13–14; Luke 13:24.

wrong. Sadly, so much of religion tells us just the opposite, and presents us with a notion of holiness very different from what Jesus models. What Jesus tells us, and perfectly models for us, is that the holiness God desires for us is that we would become like him regarding forgiveness and mercy. We may seek to be holy by being sinless, but Jesus tells us that our ambition to be sinless is both hopeless and unnecessary. God does not need us to be sinless in order to love us, since he is always able to love us through forgiveness and mercy, and, as we have said, it is only by realizing that we are the constant recipients of God's forgiveness and mercy that we come to take on his likeness in that regard. Sadly, religion, in its many forms, usually leads us in just the opposite direction.

What religion so often offers is some means by which people can see themselves as righteous or sinless, and therefore no longer in need of repentance and forgiveness. A very popular contemporary form of the Christian religion claims that our faith makes us righteous before God. Such a religion based upon righteousness, rather than forgiveness, is the very thing that Jesus so strongly opposed. Jesus constantly told the religious insiders who saw themselves as sinless that they were in need of repentance. The fact that today's religious insiders claim that their righteousness is the result of their faith rather than their ability to keep the law is of little significance. They are in the same prideful place as were the Pharisees of Jesus day. They may think that their faith has made them righteous, but a right relationship with God is always the result of God's forgiveness and mercy and not our faith. This is the gospel message: that our hope lies in the mercy of God and his great capacity for forgiveness.

It is easy to understand why people would be attracted to a religion that offers us a way to be righteous rather than simply forgiven. Our experience with human beings constantly reinforces the fact that if people are going to love us it will be because we are either good or beautiful. When we eventually become aware of God in our lives, we naturally imagine that this must be true of God as well, especially since God is supremely good and beautiful. Our human experience has taught us that good and beautiful people seek other good and beautiful people to love, and we imagine that God must do the same. Thus, we create theologies that provide hope for us becoming good or righteous in order that God might love us. Either we create a theology based upon a morality that we think we can live by, or we create a theology that tells us we are righteous because of our faith. The great error behind such theologies is that they suppose that God is like us, especially regarding love, but God is nothing like what we imagine. We imagine that sin offends God, just as it offends us. We only have a capacity to love sinless people and we imagine God must be limited in the same way. Thus, we look to theologies that offer us some way to become sinless rather than simply forgiven.

Of course, our sin does offend God, but it does not cause him to turn away from us. The idea that God cannot be in the presence of sin is the great lie. God is not like us. He meets and loves us in the midst of our sin. There is a certain sense in which God cannot be in the presence of sin, however, since our sin is that we turn away from God and fix our attention on the false gods and trivial matters of this world. When we do so, we are unaware of God's presence, but it is only in our awareness that God is not present. From our perspective, God is not present in the midst of our distractions or sins, but God is always present to us. We have turned away from God but God has not turned away from us. He is omnipresent, but we are not aware of his being present because our sin is that we are distracted from his presence.

If we fail to understand this and suppose that our sin makes it impossible for God to love us, we imagine a god very different from the God that Jesus reveals. Sadly, that is exactly what many Christians have done. They suppose that a holy God turns away from sinners, but the Scripture tells us that "God shows his love for us in that while we were yet sinners Christ died for us."[13] Still, so much of religion insists that God punishes sinners, and so much of theology attempts to give support to the belief in a punitive god. One example of such theology is a particular theory about atonement that has God the Father pouring forth his wrath upon God the Son as punishment for the sins of human beings.

Nearly all Christians believe that Jesus died for their sins, but there is grave disagreement as to what that means. Jesus says he came to be "a ransom for many."[14] He does not tell us more than that, however, and therefore several theories developed concerning the nature of the ransom. The view that dominated the early church was a theory known as *Christus Victor,* and can be traced to the early church fathers Origin and Gregory of Nyssa. In one version of *Christus Victor,* Satan held all human beings

13. Rom 5:8.
14. Matt 20:28; Mark 10:45.

captive, but God handed Jesus over to Satan as a payment or ransom for captive human beings.[15] According to this view, Satan had a right to do what he wished to human beings, and if God used violence to set Satan's captives free, "God would have been doing unjust violence against the devil, since the latter was the lawful possessor of man; for the devil had not gained his hold over man with violence rather it was man who had gone over to the devil of his own free will."[16]

Since Adam and Eve willingly enslaved themselves to the devil, their descendants were equally slaves and the property of Satan, who could do what he wished with them. With the death of Jesus, however, Satan became a murderer for the first time, since he had no legal claim to Jesus, who was born of the Holy Spirit and not descended from Adam. Another version of *Christus Victor* pictures a battle between God and the forces of evil. In the battle, God's Son gets killed but God raises him from the dead and thus defeats Satan.[17]

In the eleventh century, Anselm (A.D. 1033–1109) objected to this view and argued that the traditional idea that God had paid a ransom to Satan was a mistake as Satan had no legal claim over human beings. Neither the devil nor man belongs to anyone but God, and neither one stands outside God's power.[18] According to Anselm's theory (often referred to as the "satisfaction" or "propitiation" theory), God's honor was offended by sin and Jesus' death was necessary in order to satisfy God's offended honor. Thus, the payment is to *God* and not to Satan. Thomas Aquinas accepted a variation of this view, as did the reformers Luther and Calvin. The reformers added the idea that divine law required punishment for sin, and Jesus agreed to suffer that punishment in place of human beings.[19] In other words, Jesus was tortured in our place because God's justice requires that there is punishment for sin. Thus, Jesus suffers the wrath of God instead of us, and thereby we become guiltless because another has paid the price of our sin. This leaves us with several terrible consequences.

15. Weaver, "Violence in Christian Theology," 151.

16. Anselm, *Major Works*, 272.

17. Weaver, "Violence in Christian Theology," 151.

18. Anselm, *Major Works*, 272.

19. Weaver, "Violence in Christian Theology," 151.

First, it leaves us with a very strange notion of justice. True, justice does require that someone pay for an offense, but justice requires that the person who pays for the offense be the guilty person. If we execute an innocent person for an offense they did not commit, that would not be justice. God pouring forth his wrath upon Jesus for our sin may be a matter of God needing to release his anger or wrath upon someone but we cannot see that as somehow satisfying some sense of justice within God. The idea of the innocent suffering and the guilty going free is exactly what justice is not. That is the definition of injustice. Of course, if a person willingly suffered an offense and offered pardon rather than demanding justice, we would not think that was unjust. Indeed, if the innocent willingly suffers an offense without retaliation we are no longer talking about justice or injustice but rather forgiveness.

Another strange consequence of this atonement theory that has God pouring forth his wrath upon Jesus is that it presents us with a God who goes from hating us to loving us, and from loving Jesus to hating Jesus. This is especially strange since Christians who believe in the incarnation believe that Jesus is God, and that he and the Father are one. This theory has one person of the Christian Godhead (the Father) inflicting wrath upon another person of the Godhead (the Son). It pictures God at war within himself. If Jesus and the Father are one, then when Jesus suffers, the Father must suffer as well.

Another strange thing about this propitiation theory of atonement is that it presents us with a God whose honor is greater than his love for his Son. It pictures God as vindicating his offended honor by pouring forth his wrath upon Jesus.

By far, however, the worst consequence of the propitiation theory (and it is no more than a theory) is that it leaves us with a God with whom we could never really fall in love. If Jesus' suffering on the cross is the result of God's wrath, which God intended for us, how can we ever really fall in love with such a God? We cannot love a God who claims to love us but will torture us eternally if we do not respond properly to his love. We can certainly be obedient to such a God for fear of the kind of wrath that this theory claims God poured forth upon Jesus, but a theory that paints such a picture of God could never bring us to fall in love with him.

In order to fall in love with God, we must know that he is safe and there is nothing to fear in him. Of course, that is not where we begin. Our spiritual journey usually begins with a fear of God. Throughout the Bible, we see people falling down in fear when God or one of God's angelic messengers appears. This is our natural human response, but God's message always begins with the words, "Fear not."[20] True, all wisdom begins with a fear of God as Proverbs tells us.[21] That is where we begin the journey. When we begin the journey, however, we do not know who God is. When we do come to know him, we discover that he is our Father and nothing can separate us from his love, and that his perfect love casts out all fear. "There is no fear in love, but perfect love casts out fear; for fear has to do with punishment, and whoever fears has not reached perfection in love."[22]

The idea of Jesus paying for our sins by being tortured by God is certainly detrimental to our ever falling in love with God, but that is not the only detrimental effect of such a theory. It equally gives us reason not to love the sinner. If God does not love the sinner but requires punishment in payment for their sin, then we too can treat the sinner in a similar manner, as we become righteous and holy after what we believe to be God's likeness. If God only loves sinless, righteous people, then we too reserve our love only for the sinless. We too, in order to become holy as God is holy, pour forth our wrath upon the sinner. This was typical of the religious insiders of Jesus day, and it is typical of the religious insiders of our day. Such people are incapable of being God's agents of forgiveness and mercy. Their religious theories keep them from the gospel.

ATONEMENT AS FORGIVENESS

Certainly, Jesus does take our sin upon himself. He does pay for our sin, but not as the recipient of God's wrath. The better and more fruitful alternative to Anselm's theory is to understand that the oneness of the triune God means that when Jesus suffers on the cross, the Father suffers as well. The Father's response to our sin is the same as Jesus' response. They both suffer the pain of their creation choosing so much less than the fullness they intend for it. It is the offense and pain that a parent suffers when their child rejects so much of the blessings the parent offers them. All the persons of the Godhead suffer and pay the price that forgiveness always

20. Gen 15:1; 26:24; 46:3; Matt 1:20; Acts 27:24; Rev. 11:17 et al.

21. Prov 9:10.

22. 1 John 4:18.

entails. Jesus is not a man suffering the wrath of God in our place, but God suffering the wrath of human beings in the ultimate act of forgiveness.

Forgiveness does satisfy justice, which is so much at the heart of the satisfaction theory, but not as that theory conceives it. In its common, human form, justice requires that the guilty suffer for the harm they have done. With forgiveness, justice is satisfied in that someone does suffer and pay for the harm done: the innocent willingly chooses to suffer the offense for the sake of restoring the possibility of relationship with the guilty. Thus, the innocent makes payment on behave of the guilty. Jesus does indeed pay for our sins and justice is satisfied, but through forgiveness.

In our legal system, a third party, in the person of a judge or governor, may pardon an offender. This is very different from forgiveness, however, since the judge or governor who offers the pardon is not the offended party. Real forgiveness, the kind that restores the possibility of relationship, only occurs when the offended part pays the price by suffering the offense without retaliation. This is what Jesus so beautifully reveals from the cross. It is God willingly suffering our rejection of him, without retaliation, in order to keep open the possibility of relationship.

Not surprisingly, we human beings find the whole idea of forgiveness strange. Why would anyone want to restore a relationship with someone who hurts us? Why would anyone suffer the harm someone does to them without retaliation? When someone hurts us, our instinct is to hurt them in return—to make them suffer just as they made us suffer. There are several ways to justify our instinct to retribution. We want to make sure that we never suffer in that way again, so we think that if we hurt them in return they will learn not to hurt us again. In most cases if the hurt is serious enough, the last thing we want is to restore a relationship with that person so hurting them back assures that the relationship has ended. We think that retribution will mitigate our suffering by bringing our relationship with them to an end. We think it will bring closure to our wound. By contrast, real forgiveness is just the opposite and instead of seeking closure, forgiveness keeps open the possibility of relationship with the offender. With real forgiveness, the offended party's desire for restoration is greater than the hurt they suffered. This is the great revelation of Jesus from the Cross. As great as Jesus suffering is, God's desire for restoring relationship with us is greater than that suffering.

Christianity is all about restoring relationship through forgiveness. It begins with God's forgiveness of us and then extends to our forgiveness of others who have harmed, offended, or disappointed us. This is the most essential aspect of the Christian life, and it is what makes real Christianity so unappealing to most of us. For that reason, true followers of Jesus are rare. They are so rare that Mark Twain once quipped, "The Christian religion was a great idea, too bad no one ever tried it." Indeed, we all fall short of the kind of forgiveness to which Jesus calls us. That, however, puts us in the strangely blessed position of continually seeking forgiveness for our own lack of forgiveness, the receiving of which, ever so slowly, does make us more forgiving.

One of the worst aspects of the propitiation or satisfaction theory of atonement is that it maintains that Jesus' suffering of God's wrath has taken away our sin, and God now sees us as sinless. When we assume that Jesus has made us righteous rather than simply forgiven, we believe that we are no longer under God's judgment, and therefore no longer in need of mercy. Without the continual need to receive mercy, however, we are without the means by which we might become merciful. Instead, of becoming God's agents of mercy and forgiveness, we, like many of the Pharisees of Jesus day, find it all too easy to see the rest of the world as sinners who are under God's judgment and ourselves as righteous and loved by God.

A better understanding of Jesus' atonement is that it does not allow us to escape judgment. God does judge us, and the judgment is that we have all failed to live as Jesus lived in a constant state of prayer—a state of loving God with our whole heart, soul, mind, and strength. It is not that we are sinless, but that God confronts our sin[23] and suffers it with forgiveness for the sake of restoring or keeping open the possibility of relationship. God does not need us to be sinless in order to love us; he loves us in the midst of our sin and he wants us to become like him and take on the divine ability to love others in the midst of their sin. Our relationship with God is forever based upon his forgiveness and mercy rather than our being made sinless and therefore worthy of God's love.

Jesus' death on the cross is not one human being paying for the offense of all human beings as a penal substitute. It is rather God suffering the offense of our sin and paying for it in an act of forgiveness. From the

23. Rom 5:8.

cross, Jesus prays for his torturers to be forgiven,[24] and therein reveals the heart of God. The gospel is most essentially about forgiveness, specifically, that we would experience forgiveness in order that we would become forgiving after God's likeness. It is only appropriate that the gospel ends with the greatest possible manifestation of forgiveness; that is, with the innocent suffering the offense without retaliation in order to restore the possibility of relationship with the guilty.

In order to come into the fullness of the gospel what we need are theologies that reveal our great need of mercy and forgiveness, rather than theologies that tell us how we can be righteous before God. The latter might give us what we want but it undermines our ability to experience the ongoing forgiveness necessary to make us after his forgiving likeness. What we need is a theology that maximizes our experience of forgiveness, and for that purpose, contemplative prayer is ideally suited.

In contemplative prayer, we quickly see how we fail to give God the attention that a love relationship requires. As we attempt to focus upon God and be present, as he is present, a myriad of distractions turns our attention away from his presence, and we see how far short we fall from loving God with our whole heart, soul, mind, and strength. Such a lack of attention would cause the greatest of lovers to seek another beloved, but God always responds to our lack of love with forgiveness in order to keep open the possibility of relationship.

As we begin to practice contemplative prayer, and attempt to be present and attentive to God in the way that love requires, we quickly see what inept lovers we really are. Our failure to give God the attention that love entails, however, is the very thing that should keep us in a place of almost constant repentance, and the experience of God's never ending forgiveness. We are not forgiving and merciful creatures and our only hope of becoming such creatures is the ongoing experience of having received much forgiveness and mercy.

A theology and theory of atonement that tells us we must be guiltless in order to receive love from a god whose holiness precludes him from being in the presence of sin is a theory that undermines our transformation into his forgiving and merciful likeness. As we have said, if we believe that God's holiness precludes him from being in the presence of sin, we too will avoid being in the presence of sinners as we become holy, just as

24. Luke 23:34.

the Pharisees did. Such a theory may be very attractive to those who seek some means of seeing themselves as righteous, but it undermines God's ultimate purpose of making us into his forgiving and merciful likeness.

By contrast, if our idea of atonement is a matter of God suffering our sin in an act of forgiveness, then we too must suffer the offense of others and extend God's forgiveness and mercy, just as Jesus did. This is God's ultimate purpose: that we would become like him, not in terms of sinlessness, but in terms of forgiveness and mercy. This being God's ultimate purpose for our lives, it is no wonder that God created a world that would provide us with endless opportunities to practice forgiveness and mercy.

9

Freedom, Morality, and Judgment

As WE SAW IN the last chapter, if we are to be God's agents of forgiveness and mercy one of the great obstacles is our religious propensity toward righteousness. Religions that tell us we can be righteous through their beliefs, behaviors, or rituals do not produce people capable of being God's agents of forgiveness and mercy. Instead, they produce people who judge those whom they see as unrighteous for their lack of the right beliefs, behaviors, or rituals. Jesus calls these people hypocrites, since they claim themselves righteous but do not live by God's standard of righteousness. They may live by their religion's standard of righteousness, but Jesus tells us that no one lives by God's standard of righteousness,[1] and all are in need of mercy. Indeed, Jesus is God's standard of righteousness and we all fall short of that standard. That, however, is good news, since it puts us in a better place from which to minister to other sinners like ourselves. Unfortunately, many people who consider themselves followers of Jesus do not see that as good news and insist upon making a pretense to righteousness. Take for example, the contemporary religious debate over homosexuality.

Many contemporary Christians see homosexuality as immoral. Morality, however, requires that we are free to choose between good and evil. Animals are not moral agents since they act according to a nature

1. Luke 18:19.

81

that does not allow any freedom of choice. We consider human beings different from animals in that we are free to choose between good or evil. The sciences of the twentieth century, however, have brought the idea of human freedom into question. In light of our newfound understanding concerning genetics, as well as psychological and sociological conditioning, we now acknowledge that much of our behavior may be beyond our control. As a result, many people would argue that sexual preference is not a moral matter since it is not something we freely choose. For instance, if someone of the same sex sexually molested someone in childhood, that child may have a predilection to homosexual sex that other people do not have.

Many in the religious community take the position that sexual preference is purely a matter of choice and therefore a moral issue for which we are culpable. Both parties try to recruit Jesus to their side. Those from the religious community point to Scriptures condemning homosexuality, while the gay community points out that Jesus is silent on the matter. Of course, what Jesus does say is that our sin is not in our behavior but exists long before that, when we leave God's presence in order to fix our attention upon those things after which we lust.[2]

Thus, the religious community misses the point when they condemn homosexual behavior. The sin is in our lust long before it ever shows up in our behavior. Our lust is what possesses us and turns our attention away from an awareness of God's presence and takes us out of a state of prayer. This is our sin and heterosexual lust is just as distracting as homosexual lust. Even lust within a heterosexual marriage can be sinful if it takes us away from an awareness of God's presence. Our desire for sexual intimacy should draw us into awareness of God's presence and not away from it, but we are nearly all guilty of having our lust—either homosexual or heterosexual—cause us to ignore God's presence. Ultimately, we are all sinners and easily succumb to lusts that place us in need of repentance and a return to an awareness of the forgiving presence of God.

Some argue that heterosexual lust is natural and homosexual lust is unnatural. Thus, they equate sin with unnatural behavior. Sin, however, is part of the natural realm and not merely limited to the unnatural. We naturally wander and turn our attention from God's presence and all that he has for us in order to pursue our own desires and our own tragically

2. Matt 5:27–28.

flawed notions of happiness. We are naturally sinners and the ultimate solution that Jesus offers is not to behave one way rather than another. The morality that Jesus calls us to is the morality of a repentant heart. From Jesus' perspective, both sides in the debate over homosexuality are wrong. The homosexual is wrong in thinking that their homosexual lust is not a sin, but the heterosexual is also wrong in thinking that their heterosexual lust is not a sin. The Gospels teach us that we are all sinners. We all need to repent for the lust that takes us from an awareness of God's presence; whether it is a homosexual or heterosexual lust that distracts us is of little matter to God.

Some may not succumb to the distraction of any kind of lust, but they still may find a reason to repent for judging the sins of others or not forgiving their homosexual and heterosexual sisters and brothers for their lustful sins. What may distract them from an awareness of God's presence is their focus upon their own judgments and the sins of others. We can all find reasons to repent and return to an awareness of God's presence in prayer. The only obstacle we face is the religious belief that we are righteous and have no need of repentance.

True, this is a very different understanding of the gospel than what we usually hear from religious types. Our cultural prejudice is that religion is all about morality, and since we have made Jesus into a religion, the gospel must therefore be about morality. Of course, there is a sense in which the gospel is about morality, but the morality of which Jesus speaks is very different from what we imagine. Jesus is speaking of a morality of the heart and not a morality based in behavior. What is so interesting is that in the twenty-first century we have come to the realization that a morality of the heart maybe our only morality.

As we have said, moral agency requires freedom. Since we now know that much of our behavior is beyond our control because of genetics, or psychological and environmental conditioning, human beings may not be morally culpable for their behavior. If our behavior is much more de-termined than we had imagined, religions that claim that God rewards or punishes based upon moral behavior are seen by many twenty-first-century people as presenting an unjust God who rewards and punishes people based upon things beyond their control.

On the other hand, the other great discovery of our day is that the conceptual understanding through which we interpret the world is not

God-given or natural, but rather largely the product of human judgments and conventions passed onto us through our history, culture, and language communities. Therefore, we should realize that we are free as never before to question, reevaluate, and reconstruct the conceptual understanding through which we interpret the world.

Thus, at the same time that we came to realize that we do not have control over the genetic and environmental conditions that have such a profound influence on our behavior, we equally became aware, as never before, concerning our freedom to reinterpret our experience through alternative understandings rather than those we have inherited. Perhaps in the past, people accepted the understanding through which they interpreted the world as God-given, but we are no longer so naïve. True, we are more aware than ever about the factors that determine our behavior, but we are equally more aware than ever concerning the great liberty we possess concerning our freedom to recreate for ourselves alternative conceptual understanding very different from those that we inherit. Some have always known this. They were the intellectual giants of the past who rejected the conceptual understanding given them by their history and culture in order to come to a better understanding through which to interpret their experience.

Jesus is certainly one of those giants. He introduces us to a new way of thinking about our right relationship to God. He tells us that it is not our behavior that makes us either righteous or sinners. Righteousness and sin are much deeper than we imagine, and rooted in our hearts and minds rather than our behavior. Our real sin or offense against God lies in our hearts and minds, since none of us lives in a constant aware of God's presence the way Jesus did. None of us loves God with our whole heart, soul, mind, and strength. None of us gives God the kind of attention that love requires. This does not appear to be good news, since it means that none of us is righteous before God. There is good news, however, in the fact that just as our sin is rooted in our hearts and minds, so too is our righteousness a matter of our hearts and minds.

The Jesus prescription for enjoying the benefit of right relationship with God depends upon our having a right understanding through which to interpret our relationship with God. Following Jesus is not essentially about getting our behavior right, but about understanding that mercy and forgiveness are always the basis for our relationship with God. That, however, is very different from the concept of righteousness that we have inherited, and because of that we are in constant need of repentance; that is, a constant need to change our minds concerning our concepts of sin and righteousness.

We may have trouble changing our behavior but we can change our conceptual understanding in order that it conforms to Jesus' understanding. Since we now know that the way we have learned to understand and interpret the circumstances of our lives is not God-given but the result of human factors within our history, culture, and language communities, we are free, as never before, to reject that understanding in favor of the understanding that Jesus offers. This is real repentance, or the change of mind that is required to put us in a right understanding of our relationship with God.

Thus, a life of following Jesus is about taking on the Jesus perspective and interpreting our human condition with his conceptual understanding. To do so, we must come to conceptualize and understand sin, repentance, and forgiveness as he does. If we do take on the Jesus perspective, we will see that being right with God is not a matter of being guiltless but a matter of experiencing his forgiveness for our sin, which is much deeper than our cultural understanding has led us to believe. It is not about avoiding what we consider sins but about understanding what sin really is and responding to it with repentance.

What the gospel teaches is that those who are right with God are not those who have all of their behavior in conformity with some moral code or ethical principles. Neither is a right relationship with God based upon our having the right doctrinal beliefs. As we have been seeing throughout this text, a right relationship with God is a matter of living in an almost constant state of repentance or turning back to God and away from all of those things that so easily capture our attention and keep us from an awareness of God's presence. It is only as we repent and turn back to God and enter a state of prayer that we experience the great mystery of God's mercy and forgiveness.

If we accept this gospel perspective, then the freedom we need to be right with God is not a freedom over our behavior. All we need is a freedom to acknowledge our need to turn back toward God and repent from the thoughts and attitudes that Jesus tells us are our sin. If we listen to what Jesus has to say concerning the nature of sin and the nature of God's forgiveness, then the freedom we need to be right with God is internal and has little to do with external behavior. Rather, it is the freedom to conceptualize and interpret sin and repentance from the Jesus perspective.

True, our behavior may be beyond our complete control, but we do have the freedom to conceptualize things in a variety of ways. We can conceptualize things like sin and repentance from the Jesus perspective and choose to return at will to a state of prayer and the experience of God's forgiveness, or we can reject such a perspective and interpret things like sin and repentance from the perspective of our culture and language community. Herein lay our freedom. It is not a freedom over behavior, which we now know is unrealistic, but a freedom to conceptualize our circumstance as we choose. We generally choose the perspective of our culture and suppose that Jesus had the same concepts and understanding as our culture. We prefer our cultural understanding, and like to imagine that it is no different from Jesus understanding, since it gives us a way to judge people whose behavior and beliefs do not meet our standards, but the Jesus perspective is that we are all sinners in need of God's mercy and forgiveness.

GOD'S DESIGN FOR OUR LIVES

God desires that we would become ever more like him. That transformation into his likeness is his ultimate design for our lives. We become like Jesus, however, not by modeling his behavior. God is looking for something much deeper and more fruitful. His ultimate desire is that we would become a race of people capable of being his agents of forgiveness and mercy. In order for that to happen, as we have said, we need to become aware of receiving much forgiveness and mercy. Getting our behavior right can actually work against that purpose in that it can create the illusion that we are good, religious people and no longer in need of mercy. This does not mean that we should deliberately continue in bad behavior, but rather that from God's perspective good or bad behavior is of little consequence one way or the other. It may be of great consequence to us, but from the perspective of God's ultimate, eternal purpose, it is of little matter. What is of great matter is that we would become evermore like Jesus regarding forgiveness and mercy. The extent to which we realize this divine purpose is largely determined by how willing we are to have our minds renewed and our perspective reformed by Jesus' teachings. Those teachings center on the fact that our sin is much more than we imagine and so too is our need of forgiveness. The good news is that such an understanding should bring us into an ever-greater experience of God's forgiveness, and thereby make us evermore into his forgiving likeness.

People with good behavior do not usually see this as good news. Like many of the Pharisees of Jesus' day, good people tend to want a God who rewards their good behavior and likewise punishes bad behavior. Without having their understanding changed by Jesus teachings, people who believe that their behavior is good, and that God rewards good behavior, see no reason for repentance and therefore have little experience of God's forgiveness.

People with bad behavior have a different problem. If they believe that God rewards and punishes based upon behavior, the last thing they want is to turn to a God who they believe hates bad behavior. Thus, people, both good and bad, who believe that God is interested in behavior tend to have little experience of God's forgiveness. Either way, they fail to realize the good news, which is that God freely extends forgiveness to all who seek it. If we are to receive the good news and experience God's forgiveness, we need to understand that God is not displeased with our bad behavior, nor pleased with our good behavior. God, like the father of the prodigal is pleased with our presence and longs for nothing more than our return to his presence.[3]

Without having our perspective changed by the Jesus revelation, our judgments are all askew. We judge people who cannot get their behavior right as displeasing to God, and others who have had the cultural, social, or familial benefits that produce good behavior as pleasing to God. This is very different from the way God sees things, and we need to see human beings as God sees them.

God sees human beings as his beloved children and therefore the recipients of his love. At the same time, however, God also sees that his children are not living according to his design. They do not dwell in a constant awareness of his presence as Adam initially had in the Garden, or as Jesus had. Consequently, they do not experience the fullness of life that God has for them. In spite of this, God's love for them continues

---

3. Luke 15:11–32.

because he is willing to endure the suffering that forgiveness always entails. Furthermore, he desires that, as we experience his forgiveness we too will endure the same suffering that forgiveness always entails, and therein become his agents of forgiveness and love.

Of course, this is impossible unless we come to see that God loves us in a way that is very different from the way we love one another. We love and refuse to love based upon whether or not we see goodness in people. We love people who behave well, and do not love people who behave badly. Sadly, we all too easily imagine that God loves in the same way, and proportions his love according to our behavior, but God is very different from us. God loves all of his children. He does not love some more than others, nor does he love some less than he loves others. He longs for all of his children to return to the Garden and an awareness of his presence. We have all failed to live according to God's design, and are therefore all in need of repentance. This should bring us together in common unity. The fact that we are all in the same place of having fallen short of the kind of life that Jesus models should make us capable of loving one another in a way that is impossible with a human kind of love based upon how much goodness we find in one another. If we are to become agents of God's love, we must come to understand that our love worthiness rests solely in God's forgiveness.

FORGIVENESS, MERCY, AND JUDGMENT

If we consider the words of Jesus, it should become immediately apparent that if we are to find good news in what Jesus has to say, it must be in those things he says about forgiveness and mercy, since the standard for righteousness that he sets forth is one that none of us could ever achieve. If you are still not convinced that the Jesus standard for righteousness is so far beyond us that our only hope of being right with God lies in the greatness of God's forgiveness and mercy, consider the fact that he says, "On the day of judgment you will have to give an account for every careless word you utter; for by your words you will be justified, and by your words you will be condemned."[4] If God's judgment of us is to take into consideration every careless word we have ever uttered, we are all in

4. Matt 12:36–37.

trouble. Likewise, when we consider Jesus' other commandments to us, we see how impossible a right relationship with God is apart from his forgiveness. "Do good to those who hate you, bless those who curse you, pray for those who abuse you. If anyone strikes you on the cheek, offer the other also; and from anyone who takes away your coat do not withhold even your shirt. Give to everyone who begs from you; and if anyone takes away your goods, do not ask for them again."[5]

Surely, none of us keeps these commandments. We are all guilty when judged by the standard that Jesus sets forth, and if it were not for God's forgiveness and mercy, the Jesus message is certainly one of doom. The standard that God sets forth is that we should all live as Jesus lived, in conscious awareness of God's presence, and God's judgment is that we have all failed to live according to that design. Jesus is the fulfillment of the Law.[6] He is what it would look like if someone did live according to God's standard, but we have all failed to live the love relationship with God that Jesus lived. Unlike Jesus, who was always focused and attentive to God, our focus and attention is usually somewhere else. God made us to walk with him and be constantly aware of his presence in our lives. Adam initially had such a focused relationship and Jesus shows us what such a relationship would look like outside the Garden in a world full of distractions. Jesus commands us to follow him and live as he lived in that constant awareness of God's presence.

Of course, we have all failed to follow Jesus and live as he lived. At one point in Matthew's Gospel, the disciples of Jesus realize how impossible the standard is that he is establishing and they respond by saying, "Then who can be saved?" To which Jesus responds, "For mortals it is impossible, but for God all things are possible."[7]

This is the good news: as great as God's standard is, his mercy is even greater; in fact, it is great enough to transform us. Though his standard is that we would all live as Jesus lived, and his judgment is that we have all failed to live according to that standard, our realization of his mercy when we fail is the very thing that eventually does make us into the merciful creatures God desires us to be. The fact that we all fall short of the purpose God has for our lives certainly does not sound like good news, but it is

5. Luke 6:27–30.

6. Matt 5:17.

7. Matt 19:23–26; also see Luke 18:18–25.

good news when it makes us aware of the forgiveness and mercy he continually extends to us. The gospel is all about learning to continually seek and receive forgiveness and mercy, in order that we might become forgiving and merciful. To repeat once more, because it bears repeating, we become like him, not through our righteous moral behavior or religious practices but through our failure to live as Jesus lived, and our consequent experience of forgiveness and mercy. This is the only way for us to become forgiving and merciful, and it is only through our forgiveness and mercy that the world gets a glimpse of the divine.

The world does not necessarily see sinless, righteous behavior as divine, but it does recognize the divine in forgiving, merciful behavior. The one tells us nothing of love, but the other is the greatest expression of love. A friend of mine had a father who gave him many good memories of how much he loved his son. Most of those memories centered on the idea of forgiveness. One story he related to me was about his father having bought a new car. His father was not a wealthy man and made a living running a butcher shop. His son asked to borrow the car for a special occasion. While backing up he hit a wall and badly dented the back fender. My friend felt horrible and was terrified to tell his father. When he did manage the courage to face his father, his father responded by saying, "It's metal, we'll get it fixed." Of all the wonderful experiences my friend had with his father, his most endearing memories are those of his father's forgiveness.

We all enjoy congratulations for our successes, especially from our fathers, but no wonderful accolades from our fathers produce the degree of affection for them, as does their forgiveness. This is especially true concerning our heavenly Father. It is only through forgiveness that God endears himself to us, and we enter into the kind of love relationship he desires for us only through forgiveness. Without experiencing his forgiveness, we may be obedient to God and fearfully serve him, but we only fall in love with him through the experience of his forgiveness and mercy. In fact, the only religious experience that is ultimately worth anything is the experience of forgiveness. All other religious experiences apart from the experience of his forgiveness tend to inflate the ego and aggrandize the flesh. Only the experience of forgiveness produces the humility that is so essential to true spiritual maturity.

All this talk of forgiveness should not, however, be taken to mean that there is no judgment in God. There certainly is. There must be a judgment, and we must be aware of that judgment. Without recognizing God's judgment concerning our failure to live as Jesus lived, we would never come to experience God's forgiveness and mercy. Thus, there is a judgment in God but it is not an end for those who seek mercy. Rather God's judgment is the very thing that brings us to the experience of God's mercy. Every time we return to an awareness of God's presence in prayer, it is an experience of God's forgiveness and mercy, and we need to understand that. If we take what Jesus says about the nature of sin seriously, then every time we enter a state of prayer, we do so by turning back to God (repentance) and away from the distractions (sin) that kept us from an awareness of God's presence. Likewise, every time we return to an awareness of God's presence through repentance, he meets us with forgiveness and mercy. Thus, judgment is the very thing that leads us to repentance and union with God.

There is, however, a judgment that does not lead to repentance and union with God. For those who refuse to recognize God's judgment and their need for forgiveness, God's judgment does turn out to be an end rather than a means to forgiveness and mercy. Consequently, there is a judgment that is final, but it is not because God is limited concerning forgiveness and mercy. The final judgment is for those who neither seek mercy for themselves nor wish to become merciful toward others. For such there is final judgment. God's desire, however, is that his judgment would always lead us to repentance and the experience of his forgiveness and mercy.

The gospel is all about revealing that we have all fallen short of God's design for our lives, and how we all are in need of mercy in order that God might continue to make us into his likeness. This is what so many religious people do not get, and it is for this reason that Jesus tells the chief priests and elders of the people that they are not as righteous (i.e., right with God) as the tax collectors and the prostitutes: "Truly I tell you, the tax collectors and the prostitutes are going into the kingdom of God ahead of you. For John came to you in the way of righteousness and you did not believe him, but the tax collectors and the prostitutes believed him."[8] The way of righteousness that John preached was a righteousness

---

8. Matt 21:31–32.

of repentance. Since the tax collectors and prostitutes believed that they were in need of repentance and mercy, they opened themselves to God in a way that the religious leaders did not. The chief priests and elders, who Jesus was addressing, were trusting in their own righteousness (righteousness apart from God's mercy). They imagined that their own goodness, rather than God's forgiveness, was enough to support their relationship with God.

In that same chapter of Matthew's Gospel, Jesus goes on to say the kingdom of God will be taken away from the righteous religious leaders, "And given to a people that produces the fruits of the kingdom."[9] Those who produce fruit are not those religious people who equate fruitfulness with sinlessness. The world rightly recognizes their *self*-righteousness as righteousness that comes from their own egos rather than from God. On at least an unconscious level, we all know that Jesus is right and no one is without sin, and when someone makes the pretense to sinlessness, we recognize it as hypocrisy. By contrast, what the world does recognize as divine within human beings is forgiveness and mercy. This is why on more than one occasion when speaking to the Pharisees and religious leaders, Jesus says, "Go and learn what this means, 'I desire mercy, not sacrifice.'"[10] The Pharisees, who thought they were righteous, were questioning the righteousness of Jesus for his eating with tax collectors. Jesus tells them that it is not about their religious practices but about becoming merciful. A little while later in Matthew's Gospel, Jesus says the same thing again to the Pharisees, who question his righteousness this time for his plucking grain and eating it with his disciples on the Sabbath. Jesus says, "But if you had known what this means, 'I desire mercy and not sacrifice,' you would not have condemned the guiltless."[11]

This is typical of Jesus' encounters with the religious people of his day. The Pharisees considered themselves good people because their behavior was better than other people's behavior. Jesus message to them was that they had a very poor sense of what is good. That is still his message to religious people today who think that they are good because their behavior is better than other people's behavior. Indeed, Jesus tells us that "What

9. Matt 21:43.

10. Matt 9:13.

11. Matt 12:7.

is prized by human beings is an abomination in the sight of God,"[12] so any sense of goodness we derive by comparing ourselves to others is very different from the goodness to which God calls us. What God desires is that we would compare ourselves with Jesus, and the standard that he sets forth, and in so doing, we would see our great need of God's mercy.

Many people, however, imagine that they can sustain a relationship with God based upon their own righteous behavior. There is a great story that exemplifies this in Luke's Gospel. In the tenth chapter of Luke's Gospel, a man approaches Jesus and asks what he must do in order to gain eternal life. Jesus typically responds by refusing to answer but instead asks the man a question, saying, "What is written in the Law?"[13] The man answered, "You should love the Lord your God with all your heart, and with all your soul, and with all of your strength, and with all your mind; and your neighbor as yourself."[14] Jesus affirms his answer, but wanting to justify himself, the man asked Jesus, "And who is my neighbor?"[15] Jesus responds by telling the story of the Good Samaritan: "A man was going down from Jerusalem to Jericho, and fell into the hands of robbers, who strip him, beat him, and went away, leaving him for dead. Now by chance a priest was going down that road; and when he saw him, he passed by on the other side. So likewise a Levite, when he came to the place and saw him, passed by on the other side. But a Samaritan while traveling came near him; and when he saw him, he was moved with pity."[16] Jesus goes on to tell how the Samaritan bandaged the man's wounds, took him to an inn and paid for his keep until he was well. Jesus then asks, "Which of these three . . . was a neighbor to the man who fell into the hands of the robbers?"[17] The man answers correctly and Jesus tells him to "go and do likewise."[18]

The point is that God's purpose for our life is much greater than we imagine, and so too is our sin or failure to fulfill that purpose much greater than we imagine. That is the point of almost all of Jesus' teach-

---

12. Luke 16:15.

13. Luke 10:26.

14. Luke 10:27.

15. Luke 10:29.

16. Luke 10:30–33.

17. Luke 10:34.

18. Luke 10:37.

ings. Although we think that we are good because we avoid murder or adultery, Jesus points out that what God desires is that we become, like the Samaritan, the agents of God's mercy. This is God's design, but we choose not to follow that design. This is the offense of the priest and the Levite in the story about the Samaritan. They are indeed sinners, not because of what they did, but because they are not producing "the fruits of the kingdom,"[19] which are namely forgiveness and mercy.

Jesus is constantly pointing out the sins of people who think they are sinless, and praising those who the religious people saw as sinners. The only two people whose faith Jesus praises are a Roman centurion[20] and the Canaanite woman.[21] Both were outside the religious establishment of Jesus day. Indeed, the religious establishment of Jesus' day considered both sinners. What both had in common, however, was their faith in some higher authority. Both believed that their fate was determined from above rather than by their own behavior. The religious people, on the other hand, believed that they determined their own fate through their righteous behavior.

Jesus' teachings consistently confirm that blessing comes to us, not in response to our goodness, but because of God's goodness. This was an offense to the good, religious people of Jesus day, just as it is an offense to many religious types today. Good, religious people insist upon believing that God rewards good behavior or right beliefs and punishes evil behavior or wrong beliefs. In the above story of the Samaritan, the priest and Levite pass by because they lack mercy; but part of that lack of mercy stems from a religious belief that evil comes our way in life as a result of our sin, just as blessings are a result of our goodness. Thus, the man on the side of the road is in the state he is in because of his sin. Jesus is constantly addressing this common notion in order to show us how wrong it is.

At the base of almost all religions is the supposition that God wants us to be good, but Jesus tells us that God knows that we are not good. God alone is good, and our relationship with God will always depend upon his goodness and not our own. This is what both the Roman centurion and the Canaanite woman understood: that what happens to them is not because of them but because of something above them. By contrast, this is

19. Matt 21:43.
20. Luke 7:2–9.
21. Matt 15:22–28.

what the religious men in the story of the Good Samaritan do not understand. They think that what happens to us is because of us being good or
bad, but the truth is something way beyond that. Perhaps it is something
beyond our understanding, but what we can understand is that it is not
about our being good but about us becoming like him concerning mercy
and forgiveness. If we could ever come to accept that, it would give us a
very different understanding of God's judgment. The intention of God's
judgment is not to separate us from God but to draw us into the experience of his forgiveness.

Jesus says there is a narrow way and few find it.[22] The reason it is so
hard to find is that it takes us in the opposite direction from the broad way
of moral and religious goodness that most pursue. Indeed, unlike most
who strive to be good, the ones who truly become forgiving and merciful do so by seeing that they are not good and are continually in need of
forgiveness and mercy. Those who continue to cry out for forgiveness and
mercy, because they know they are not living the way Jesus calls them to
live, are, in fact, on the right path to becoming merciful. This is why Jesus
is always pointing out that the sinners, who understand their need for forgiveness and mercy, are moving in the right direction, while the Pharisees
and other *good* people, who think they have no need of mercy, are moving
in the wrong direction.

Many of today's Christians are just such people. They may think that
they avoid the Pharisaic mode by claiming that their righteousness is not
because of their moral or religious practices, as was the righteousness of
the Pharisees, but because of their faith in Christ. However, it is still their
profession of faith, and not God's ongoing mercy, that they believe lies at
the base of their relationship with God. Many of today's Christians believe
themselves to be the same kind of insiders that the Pharisees believed
themselves to be, but the message of the gospel is that we are all sinners.
We are all outsiders in need of mercy.

Still, religious people never tire of coming up with arguments that
show that they are right with God because of what they have done. One
very popular ploy is to use the Scripture that tells us that, "If you confess
with your mouth that Jesus is Lord and believe in your heart that God
raised him from the dead, you will be saved."[23] Their hope is that this

---

22. Matt 7:14.

23. Rom 10:9.

Scripture will trump the hard teachings of Jesus. Of course, Jesus says that whoever "believes in me will also do the works that I do and, in fact will do greater works than these."[24] From this it seems obvious that none of us believe in him as we should, lest we would be doing the works that he did, and even greater works than he did. Works are the obvious evidence of our beliefs. If I tell you of a certain stock that I believe will enormously increase in value, but I have not invested any of my own money in that stock, you would be right to question whether I really did believe in that stock. When we compare our own lives to that of Jesus, it seems obvious that none of us believes, or we would be doing the things that Jesus did, namely perpetually seeking God's presence rather than being distracted by just about anything. The fact that we so easily are distracted from an awareness of God's presence should be evidence enough that none of us believes as we should, and we all need God's mercy rather than faith in our own beliefs.

We may begin the journey Jesus calls us to by believing that, "If [we] confess with [our] mouth that Jesus is Lord and believe in [our] heart that God raised him from the dead, [we] will be saved."[25] That can certainly be a good first step that can lead us into God's design and purpose for our lives, but it is only a first step. Jesus is not yet Lord, nor are we living as he lived in a constant awareness of his Father's presence. Of course, we never reach that end or purpose for our lives. It is always out beyond us, but our failure to achieve that end is the very thing that puts us in a place to receive God's ongoing forgiveness and mercy, which does accomplish God's ultimate purpose. God makes us into his likeness, as we have repeatedly said, not by us doing it right but by us doing it wrong and experiencing the greatness of God's forgiveness and mercy.

Unfortunately, many Christians today have a theology that undermines this design that God has for our lives. Their theology prevents them from seeing themselves as the ongoing recipient of forgiveness and mercy. As such, they, like the Pharisees before them, do not become agents of God's forgiveness and mercy. They are content to know that God loves them and they are going to heaven, but they are not interested in anything beyond that. Sadly, many who consider themselves followers of Jesus are in just such a place. In order to get beyond that place and come into

24. John 14:12.
25. Rom 10:9.

the fullness of life God has for us, we need deeper experiences of God's forgiveness and mercy, and such experiences only come with our failed attempts at practicing his presence. Only as we attempt to spend time in an awareness of God's presence do we see how little we love God and how easily we are distracted, and must always depend upon his forgiveness to keep his presence available to us.

10

The Problem of Evil

WHAT PHILOSOPHERS AND THEOLOGIANS refer to as "the problem of evil" results from the fact that if God is all-good, all-knowing, all-powerful, and the sole creator of the universe, how do we explain the existence of evil? This creates what logicians call inconsistency. We can resolve the inconsistency by removing any one of the above-mentioned attributes of God. If God were not all-good there would obviously be evil in the world because of the evil in the creator. Likewise, if God were not all-knowing he could have created a world that he thought would be free of evil without knowing that evil would result from his creation. Equally, we could understand God to be less than all-powerful. In Plato's *Timaeus*, the character Timaeus claims that the Demiurge who created the world tried to eliminate all of the preexisting evil but was not powerful enough to do so. Another alternative is to imagine that God was not the sole creator of the universe. According to the ancient Persian religion of Zoroastrianism, there were two creators: one good and one evil, hence the existence of evil.

Christian orthodoxy has always dealt with this problem by trying to explain evil and suffering in a way that resolves the inconsistency without eliminating any of the divine attributes. Some have argued that evil is only apparent and not ultimately real. Things may appear evil to us but that is to perceive things from our limited perspective; it is to view things in light of what we like or do not like. If we could see things from God's eternal perspective, we would see them very differently. Unfortunately, the result of such a position is that it tends to make us less than compassionate. When people are suffering, if we believe that the evil they suffer is only apparent and not ultimately real, we will tend to lack the very important virtue of compassion. Jesus extended true compassion to people suffering the evil of this world, and he calls us to do the same. A diminished capacity for compassion is a high price to pay for exonerating God as the source of evil.

Over the centuries, philosophers and theologians have proposed a host of other possible ways to explain or justify the existence of evil, but the one I find most compelling is the idea of evil as instrumental. John Hick, in his book *Evil and the God of Love*, claims that what we call evil is a necessary ingredient in God's purpose of making us into his likeness. Hick claims that God has made us in his image and likeness,[1] but although we bear the image of God from birth, the likeness of God takes a lifetime to develop. In that process, God uses what we call evil as an instrument to that purpose. Just as a medical operation might be painful and undesirable in itself, it can have the consequence of restoring us to health. Likewise, God uses what we find painful and undesirable to make us into the Divine likeness.

Hick, like most people, thinks that the way God perfects us and makes us into his likeness is largely a matter of perfecting our moral behavior. His position on evil as instrumental is even more convincing, however, if we understand that the divinization God calls us to is not in terms of being sinless but in terms of becoming his agents of forgiveness and mercy. If we understand God perfecting us into the divine likeness by becoming evermore forgiving rather than sinless, the existence of evil is perfectly consistent with an all-good, all-knowing, and all-powerful sole creator. If what it means to follow Jesus is a matter of becoming agents of God's forgiveness and mercy, it makes sense that God would create a world that would give us the greatest possible opportunity to develop those divine attributes. If we are to become loving, as God is loving, and extend our love to sinners and even our enemies[2] through forgiveness and mercy, it makes sense that God would create a world full of sinners and

---

1. Gen 1:26.

2. Jesus washes the feet of Judas (John 13:2–5), and prays from the cross for his torturers would be forgiven in order that they might spend eternity with him (Luke 23:34).

enemies in order to give us the greatest possible opportunity to develop into his forgiving likeness.

Of course, we do not want a God whose purpose for our lives is to transform us into people who can love sinners and enemies. We want God to be a moral cop, who enforces divine justice, which we imagine is a matter of rewarding good behavior and punishing bad behavior. We want God to be the enforcer of the kind of order we would want if we were God. If we were God, we would base our sovereignty upon power and reward those who obey us and punish those who dare to disobey. The God that Jesus reveals, however, bases his sovereignty upon forgiveness and love. The Jesus revelation is that of a loving God who desires to produce love within his creation. His great purpose behind creation is to create people who, like himself, are able to change others, not through the threat of force, but through forgiveness and love. In order to accomplish that purpose, we must participate by becoming evermore aware of the forgiveness he constantly extends to us.

Jesus tells us that, "The one to whom little is forgiven, loves little."[3] Conversely, to love much, we must experience much forgiveness. We usually understand this to mean that the one with the greater sin will receive a greater degree of forgiveness and therefore will love more, but that is a wrong way to understand the idea of receiving much forgiveness. We are forgetful creatures and no matter how great our offense might be, in no time, we forget its gravity and the greatness of the forgiveness we received. In fact, Jesus tells a story to illustrate this fact. He tells us of an unforgiving servant who, after his master has forgiven him a great deal, did not forgive another who owed him a very small amount.[4] Like all of Jesus parables, he is not telling us about a particular unappreciative individual. He is instead relating a universal truth that applies to almost all of us. We are all forgetful of others having forgiven us, and acutely aware of the offenses we have suffered. The only way to correct this and make us into people who realize the greatness of the forgiveness we have received is to experience forgiveness on an almost constant basis. By constantly being aware of receiving forgiveness, we do, in time, become more forgiving ourselves and respond to others with forgiveness rather than a demand for justice. Thus, the one who habitually receives forgiveness is more likely to become forgiving

3. Luke 7:47.
4. Matt 18:23–35.

than the one who experiences a single, great act of forgiveness that all too easily slips from consciousness.

This is the great problem with imagining that God forgives us in one act of atonement for all time, and never again suffers the offense of our sin. If Jesus suffered the offense of our sin, once, and God does not continually suffer the offense of our sin, then we have no continual need of repentance, and likewise no continual source from which to experience God's forgiveness. The truth is that God continues to suffer our rejection of him, and we continually need to repent and experience his forgiveness for our failure to love God the way Jesus calls us to love him with our whole heart, soul, mind, and strength.

In order to understand this, we must see that we grieve the heart of God long before any evil behavior appears. Likewise, God's desire is that we would repent and turn back to an awareness of God's presence, not when our behavior becomes evil, but every time we find ourselves distracted from an awareness of his presence. God's desire is that we would all live the way Jesus lived; that is, in a constant awareness of the Father's presence. Whenever we leave such a state of prayer, we need to turn back or repent. Our culture may imagine that the sins that separate us from God are things like murder or adultery, but Jesus was sinless not because he avoided such behaviors, but because he was never distracted from an awareness of his Father's presence. Throughout the Gospels, Jesus offers many teachings in order to reveal sins that our culture finds difficult to see as sinful. In the story of the Great Banquet,[5] the reason that people chose not to come to the feast was not that they chose instead to be at a crack house or bordello, but because they were doing business or getting married. We assume there is nothing wrong with doing business or getting married, but Jesus tells us that anything that keeps us from the great banquet God has for us is cause for repentance. Indeed, we are almost all kept from the fullness of life that God has for us by innocuous activities that occupy us in ways that keep us from an awareness of God's presence.

Jesus is constantly pointing out that the standard to which God is calling us is much greater than we would like to imagine, and that there is a judgment. The judgment is that we have all failed to live in the fullness of life that God intends for us. The purpose of the judgment, however, is not to condemn us but to bring us to repentance in order that we might

5. Luke 14:16–24.

experience God's forgiveness. We have all gone our own way, and sought to find life and meaning apart from God. Our sin is that our hearts are prone to wander, but it is the recognition of that which causes us to return to an awareness of God's presence through repentance, and the experience of God's forgiveness.

At this point, we should better understand why an all-good and all-powerful creator would fashion a world where human beings would constantly be tempted to go off on their own to seek life and meaning apart from God. It is only in a world where the opportunity for sin and all the evil that follows from it is abundant, that there is equally the opportunity to come to know the greatness of God's forgiveness and mercy. Such a world provides countless opportunities to both receive forgiveness from God and to practice our divine likeness by extending forgiveness to others.

We may find it strange that God would create a world so ripe with evil, but that is because we equate evil with pain and suffering, the absence of which we consider happiness. Jesus, however, points to a deeper, richer, and more divine happiness. The happiness he has for us draws us into the pain and suffering that is so much a part of forgiveness and love. We find this hard to understand. We want God to be who we would be if we were God. If we were God, we would destroy those portions of creation that did not immediately conform to our idea of what is good. We would punish the prodigal son and reward the good son.[6] We, like Jonah, would have God punish evil and eliminate those people who are unlike us in their morality or theology. We understand neither God's love, nor his ultimate purpose behind creation, and therefore we do not understand his tolerance of evil. True, there are places in Scripture where God does seem to sanction violence in order to eliminate evil, but his desire is always to transform evil through forgiveness. Henri Nouwen puts it best: "If evil is seen only as an irreversible, clearly visible, and sharply outlined tumor, then there is only one possibility: cut it out. And then violence is necessary. But when evil is reversible and can be turned into good through forgiveness, then nonviolence become possible."[7]

God's desire is always for transformation through forgiveness, and it is for that reason that God is so tolerant of evil. Indeed, God tolerates

6. Luke 15:11–32.

7. Nouwen, *Encounters with Merton*, 102.

evil and is "kind to the ungrateful and the wicked,"[8] not simply because they are his creation—his beloved sons and daughters—but because God knows that the ungrateful and the wicked might be the very ones with the greatest potential to realize God's ultimate purpose. That is, they may have the greatest potential to become the forgiving and merciful likeness of Jesus. God knows that often the greatest sinner makes the greatest saint, and that we ultimately come to know who God is not by doing it right but by doing it wrong. We see many examples of this throughout Scripture: Moses, David, and Paul are murders or accomplices to murder, and yet God uses them because they come to know God in a way that most of us never do. Likewise, in the genealogy of Jesus, of the five women mentioned, one is an adulterous, one a prostitute, and another pretends to be a prostitute in order to get pregnant from her own father-in-law. There is something about doing it wrong that makes us understand God's heart in a way that we never understand by doing it right. The father in the story of the prodigal loves the good, older son as much as the prodigal, but the prodigal comes to understand the father's love in a way that the good, older son never does.

In that same fifteenth chapter of Luke's Gospel where Jesus tells the story of the Prodigal Son, he tells another parable about the Lost Sheep. At the end of that parable Jesus says, "I tell you that in the same way there will be more rejoicing in heaven over one sinner who repents than over ninety-nine righteous persons who do not need to repent."[9] If the gospel were about doing it right, why would there be more rejoicing over someone that did it wrong rather than those that do it right and had no need of repentance? What is so wonderful about repentance that there is rejoicing in heaven? There are probably many reasons for the rejoicing in heaven over the repentant sinner, but one is that only the repentant sinner knows who God is. We discover the truth of God's divine, forgiving nature only through repentance, and the personal experience of his forgiveness.

Of course, this does not mean that we should indulge in sinful behavior in order to experience God's forgiveness. That is not necessary since our sin occurs, and we grieve the heart of God, long before any evil behavior appears. Consequently, we are ripe with opportunities for repentance and the experience of God's forgiveness.

8. Luke 6:35.

9. Luke 15:7.

We should not take all this talk to mean that we are not to oppose evil, however. Evil is to be opposed, but our opposition to evil should always be with compassion. We should oppose evil, but always with the kind of compassion that will lead the sinner to repentance and the experience of God forgiveness. The hope and purpose of our confrontation of evil, whether in others or ourselves, should always be intent upon bringing about the experience of God's forgiveness in order that we become ever-more like him. In order to do that, we must oppose evil and the suffering it produces in a very different way than that to which human beings have become accustomed. Jesus did not come into the world to destroy evil and suffering, but to show us how we can divinely transform it through forgiveness.

INCARNATIONAL MYSTICISM

The real key to understanding the problem of evil is to understand the incarnation. God not only created a world that abounds with evil and suffering, but he entered into that world in order to show us how to become like him in terms of forgiveness and love. This is the great mystery of incarnation. I know some atonement theories have tried to end that mystery, and explain atonement as a matter of God punishing Jesus for our sin, but the revelation of Jesus on the cross is the revelation of a God who transforms evil by suffering it and releasing it through forgiveness. This is the divine revelation of the cross; and those that have taken it seriously, and have followed Jesus to their own crosses by suffering evil and releasing it through forgiveness, have found themselves become a little more like God.

There is something so divinely beautiful about God entering into the suffering of the world that it confounds our understanding, but although our understanding may not comprehend it, we can experience it ourselves by entering into the suffering of others. Think of the person you love most in this world and recall the times when you felt closest to them—when you felt that closeness that goes beyond what we normally feel as human beings. It is most always a time of suffering. Nothing brings us together like suffering. Great suffering and great love are the things that transform us, and they are often experienced together.

Sadly, this is not the message we all too often hear from religious people. Instead, they tell us that righteousness is about confronting evil with violence and eliminating it rather than transform it. What we hear from many religious people is that God hates evil and the suffering it causes, and obedient followers of God should do everything in their power to eliminate it. What is behind such thinking is the idea of holiness as sinlessness. That was certainly the Pharisees notion of holiness, but Jesus tells us that holiness is very different from what the Pharisees imagined. Jesus' notion of being holy, as God is holy, is a matter of being forgiving and merciful, and that kind of holiness only comes through an ever-greater experience of God's forgiveness and mercy, and that only through an increased awareness of the depth of our sin.

There have always been these two very different notions of holiness. Unfortunately, the pharisaic notion of holiness as sinlessness is the more common, while the kind of holiness of Jesus speaks of is always more rare. Rare as it may be, however, we can still see that kind of holiness in those individuals who are conscious of the depth of their sin, and consequently live in an almost constant state of repentance and the experience of God's forgiveness and mercy. These are our saints and God's agents who in every generation continue to bring Christ's love to the world.

11

The Saint

GOD IS VERY DIFFERENT from what we imagine. We imagine a god whose goodness would eliminate all evil, but Jesus reveals a God who, rather than eliminating evil with violence, suffers it willingly and then transforms it through forgiveness. This is the ultimate fulfillment of the Law—the ultimate elimination of evil through forgiveness. This is the great revelation of the cross. It is the revelation of something so divinely beautiful that, if we really take it in, we fall in love with the God that Jesus reveals. The saint is one who has received this revelation and allowed herself to fall in love with God. This is the ultimate end of prayer. Remember the first picture of prayer that we offered was that of falling *in love* and giving the kind of attention that lovers give to their beloved. It is having the one we love always in our thoughts. This is great prayer: that we focus our attention on the Great Presence that is God and want nothing to distract us from that focus.

Most people never really fall in love with God. They may say that they love God, but they are certainly not *in love* with God. God is not in all of their thoughts nor do they sense a constant need to fix their thoughts upon him, as only lovers do. For most of us, our attention is always on the distractions and not on God. We are not *in love* with God because we have never really taken in the beauty of the gospel. We may say we are followers of Jesus, but the Jesus we follow is the powerful, miraculous Jesus that raises the dead, heals the blind and crippled, and walks on water. We can follow that Jesus, and many do, but we can never really fall in love with that Jesus. If we decide to become a disciple because we see power in the one we wish to follow, it is not love that makes us disciples but a respect or fear of power. For many religious types, that is enough. Certainly, we almost all begin there, but God is always calling us on into a deeper love relationship. We may begin with a fear of God and the Scripture tells us that "fear of the Lord is the beginning of wisdom,"[1] but that is just a beginning, and "Perfect love casts out fear."[2]

We get to that place of perfect love—that place of being *in love* with God—not by obedience to God's commands out of fear of hell and the promise of heaven, but by beholding the beauty of the God that Jesus reveals. Augustine called it the beatific vision, and it is only that vision of just how beautiful the Jesus revelation is that really brings us into the deep love-relationship with God that is prayer. Without the beatific vision that is the Jesus revelation, we may develop a contemplative practice of being present, but unless we fall in love, we are doing it out of our own discipline and not out of the *in love* relationship to which God calls us. Most of us are not ready for either an *in love* relationship with God or deep prayer, so we settle for obeying and serving God but pull up short of being *in love* with him. We do not like the sense of being out of control that comes with being *in love*, so we never really allow the beatific vision of the gospel to seduce us. We guard our hearts, and keep God at a distance, but without falling *in love* with God, we can never give him the kind of attention that both love and prayer require. Without falling *in love* with God, prayer will never be the constant returning of our attention to the God that possesses our conscious as only a lover can.

In spite of our general reluctance to fall *in love* with God, in every generation, some do behold the beatific vision; they see the beauty of the gospel, and fall in love with the God that Jesus reveals. When they do, they find that a divine presence possesses their consciousness. They have become intoxicated with an awareness of God's presence and the distractions of the world have less hold upon them than upon the rest of us. We call them saints.

Having been raised a Catholic, I knew of the saints. Saints were people who the Church was sure were in heaven. Furthermore, saints

1. Ps 111:10.
2. 1 John 4:18.

were also people who were very different from the rest of us while here on earth. Years later, I became a born-again Christian and evangelicals told me that all Christians were saints. All Christians were going to heaven and all Christian were different from the rest of humanity. That made sense to me then but thirty years later things appear quite different. When I consider the matter today, the saint does appear to be very different from the rest of us.

We are familiar in our culture with the idea of some people being different from the rest of us. In our contemporary American culture, the celebrity is such an individual. The reason for their being different is that mass media gives the celebrity a notoriety that goes way beyond that of the average person. Since the celebrity is identifiable by a great multitude of people, their identity appears to be more substantial than the rest of us who are only identifiable by that handful of people who make up our rather small world. Certainly, this idea that some people's identity is greater than others because they are identifiable by more people is an illusion, but it is an illusion deeply entrenched in contemporary culture.

In fact, this illusion that the celebrity has a greater identity than the rest of us is so deeply entrenched in our social reality that it should not be surprising that we have replaced the idea of the saintly Christian with the idea of the celebrity Christian. Evidence of this is all around us. At a recent local prayer breakfast, the guest speaker was a movie star who had, two years previously, had a conversion experience. They chose him because many people would be interested in his testimony, not because of his saintliness, but because of his celebrity. Many churches that have extensive standards for a person to be a ministering member, ironically would invite a celebrity to their pulpit with little reservation. Some time ago, I voiced a disagreement to something a television preacher was saying. My mother-in-law's response was that I was not on TV, and he was. Obviously, his opinion was more authoritative, not because of what he said but because of his celebrity. Go to any bookstore and you will see that celebrities make up the vast majority of those who are authoring books that purport to instruct us in the Christian life. Publishers know that in order to sell great quantities of books, the author has to be identifiable by a great many people. Consequently, television preachers, sports stars, and every other imaginable celebrity are the ones from whom we take our spiritual direction. Sadly, their spiritual authority comes from their celebrity rather than their saintliness. Our culture has taught us that what we should revere about a person is the fact that they have an identity established by a great many people. Thus, baseball players tell us what coffee to drink and movie stars what credit card to use. How strange! It is, however, more than simply strange when celebrities are the ones we look to in order to understand how to follow Jesus.

It is especially strange that the celebrity has replaced the saint in our culture because the celebrity is the complete opposite of the saint. While the celebrity draws their identity from the notoriety that masses of people provide, the saint draws her identity from God alone. Unlike the celebrity, and all who desire to be celebrities and have their identities established by great numbers of people, the saint rejects such an identity and seeks only to be who God says they are, no more and no less. The saint repeatedly turns from the identity others attempt to impose upon her and only identifies herself as God's beloved daughter. The saint sees the notoriety and prestige that the celebrity has and the rest of us seek as the illusion that it is. It is an illusion because the masses of people who serve to provide the celebrity with their identity have no real knowledge of who the celebrity actually is. Since our identity is largely the result of our relationship and interaction with others, an identity founded upon our relationship with people who really do not know us is the least substantial identity. The celebrity's identity may have the illusion of being more substantial because a great multitude of people establishes that identity, but they are people without any personal knowledge of the celebrity.

By contrast, the saint's identity appears to be the least substantial since it rests upon the saint's relationship with one person alone. It is, however, our only true source of identity, since that one person is the only one who does truly know us. This is what makes the saint so different not only from the celebrity, but from the rest of us as well. While we form an identity out of our relationships with those people who make up our small worlds, and the celebrity out of their relationship with the masses, the saint's identity is rooted in the only one whose notice really matters.

It is not easy to maintain such a saintly focus even if one has an intimate and defining relationship with God. That is because it is easy to slip into the identity others impose upon us rather than who we are in God. It is easy because for most of us what others know about us is our good, moral behavior, our charitable acts, and our attempts at fruitful ministries.

We like to think of ourselves the way others think of us because we have fooled them into believing that we are the false self we have created. God, however, identifies us at our core of who we really are. At our core, we are God's creation rather than our own. This is what the saint understands but it is difficult for the celebrity or anyone with what our culture sees as a substantial identity to realize such an identity in God. In fact, the more apparently substantial our identity is the more difficult it is to establish an identity in God.

Aristotle said that a substance (*ousia*), was that which existed independent of all else. Unlike qualities (blue), quantities (seven), and relations (father), which are dependent upon the substance they modify, a substance is more real because it is independent in a way that qualities, quantities, and relations are not. In our culture, the idea of being substantial carries that same idea of independence. Substantial people are independent people, but saintly people are just the opposite. They are dependent upon God for everything, while substantial people are dependent upon no one but themselves. I think it is for this reason more than any other that so much of Jesus' teachings are against wealth.

In Jesus day, there was no mass media and so there were no celebrities, as we know them today. What gave individuals in the ancient world a substantial identity was wealth, and it is for that reason that Jesus preaches so strongly against wealth. Like the celebrity of today, those in the ancient world who possessed wealth received the admiration of others and drew their identity from it rather than God. The ancient world saw those with such substantial identities as the fortunate or blessed ones, but Jesus tells us that they are not the fortunate ones. In fact, it seems that wealth, and the identity it produced, is not a blessing at all. In the parable of the Rich Man and Lazarus, Jesus says,

> There was a rich man who was dressed in purple and fine linen and who feasted sumptuously every day. And at his gate lay a poor man named Lazarus, covered with sores, who longed to satisfy his hunger with what fell from the rich man's table; even the dogs would come and lick his sores. The poor man died and was carried away by the angels to be with Abraham. The rich man also died and was buried. In Hades, where he was being tormented, he looked up and saw Abraham far away with Lazarus by his side. He called out "Father Abraham, have mercy on me, and send Lazarus to dip the tip of his finger in water and cool my tongue; for I am in

agony in these flames." But Abraham said, "Child, remember that during your lifetime you received your good things, and Lazarus in like manner evil things; but now he is comforted here, and you are in agony. Besides all this, between you and us a great chasm has been fixed, so that those who might want to pass from here to you cannot do so, and no one can cross from there to us."[3]

In this parable, it is not clear why this rich man is being tormented, nor does Jesus say that God is the one tormenting him. What Jesus does tell us is that the man was rich and lived well when he was alive. So is the point of the parable that riches are the cause of his torment? That is certainly not the perspective of most television ministries nor is it the perspective of American politicians who have incorporated religion into their political platforms. According to their reading of the gospel, God blesses us with wealth. That, however, is very different from what Jesus preached. Jesus very specifically tells us not to store up treasure on earth: "Do not store up for yourselves treasures on earth, where moth and rust destroy, and where thieves break in and steal. But store up for yourselves treasures in heaven, where moth and rust do not destroy, and where thieves do not break in and steal. For where your treasure is, there your heart will be also."[4]

In other places, Jesus is even more critical of wealth. In Luke's Gospel, Jesus says, "Woe to you who are rich, for you have received your consolation."[5] Likewise, in the parable of the Sower and the Seed, which appears in all three of the Synoptic Gospels, Jesus tells us that the seed that "was sown among thorns, this is the one who hears the word, but the cares of the world and the lure of *wealth* [my emphasis] choke the word, and it yields nothing."[6] Jesus also tells us in the Synoptic Gospels, "it is easier for a camel to go through the eye of a needle than for someone who is rich to enter the kingdom of God,"[7] and in Luke's Gospel, he presents us with a parable about a man who sought wealth rather than God.

The land of a rich man produced abundantly. And he thought to himself, "What should I do, for I have no place to store my crops?"

3. Luke 16:19–26.

4. Matt 6:19–21 NIV.

5. Luke 6:24.

6. Matt 13:22; also see Mark 4:19; Luke 8:14.

7. Matt 19:24; also see Mark 10:23–25; Luke 18:24.

Then he said, "I will do this: I will pull down my barns and build larger ones, and there I will store all my grain and my goods. And I will say to my soul, Soul, you have ample goods laid up for many years; relax, eat, drink, be merry." But God said to him, "You fool! This very night your life is being demanded of you. And the things you have prepared, whose will they be?" So it is with those who store up treasures for themselves but are not rich toward God.[8]

Jesus' point is that we can find security and rest in God alone, and to try to find it anywhere else is both idolatrous and foolish. Jesus also points out the idolatrous nature of wealth when he tells us that we cannot serve two masters. He says very specifically that the two masters are God and wealth: "No one can serve two masters; for a slave will either hate the one and love the other, or be devoted to the one and despise the other. You cannot serve God and wealth."[9]

It is hard to find another subject against which Jesus so adamantly preaches. His teachings against sexual immorality do not compare with his teachings against wealth. Strange that we do not admit homosexuals into our churches but rich men are welcome in spite of all of Jesus' teachings. Of course, the foundation of our society is wealth or capital. So how do we resolve the teachings of Jesus with a culture deeply rooted in the value of wealth?

Apologists for our socio-economic system are quick to quote Paul and argue that it is the *love* of money that is evil, and therefore not money itself.[10] There may be some truth to this since poor people can love wealth and lust after it even in its absence. The poor can worship money, just as the powerless can lust after power, and the nobodies can dream of being somebody. Such things can still be the idols we worship even when we have no access to them. Thus, if it is the love of money that is evil and not money itself, we can easily define or understand love in a way that does not describe our relationship to money. Although it might be easy to convince ourselves that we do not *love* money, it is not so easy to convince ourselves that we do not identify with money, and allow it to define us. As we have seen, our identity is to be in God alone, but in the world in which we live, the thing that identifies and defines us is money.

8. Luke 12:16–21.

9. Matt 6:24.

10. 1 Tim 6:10.

In a capitalistic culture, money is the way we measure the worth or value of a thing. In addition to being a means of exchange and a source of surplus (capital), the other function of money is that it serves as a measure of value. How good is that suit or car? The monetary price tells us its worth. Likewise, a person's wealth tells us the worth of that person. Of course, this is an illusion but we can easily be caught up in it and measure other human beings and ourselves by such a standard. The illusion of wealth, like that of celebrity, easily entangles us and keeps us from the fullness of life God has for us. Just as celebrity can give us a false sense of value and identity apart from God, so too does wealth.

The saintly solution to this dilemma is not what we might think. True, we may picture the saint as a reclusive ascetic who avoids both notoriety and possessions, but that is not necessarily the Jesus solution. Jesus prescribes the same solution for all sin. The solution is repentance. As with the rest of Jesus' teachings, his teachings on wealth are intent upon bringing us to repentance in order that we might seek and receive forgiveness, and thereby become forgiving after his likeness.

This is what the saint understands and equally what makes them so different from the rich and celebrated. What makes them different is not that their pious nature makes them immune to the pull of such strong idols. It is quite the opposite. Unlike the rest of us, the saint is more acutely aware of the sinister nature of the idols of this world and therefore lives in a more constant state of repentance and turning back toward God. The saint is different from the rest of us, not in their being sinless, but in their awareness of their sin and need of repentance. Unlike the self-righteous who try to cover or excuse their sin in order to appear sinless, the saint exposes her sin in order that she might become ever more aware of God's forgiveness and love. While most of us seek righteousness, the saint sees much more clearly the depth of her sin. Her acute awareness of her sin is what produces a saintly humility that is very different from the pride that comes from seeing ourselves as righteous. Unlike the rest of us who seek to be bigger and more substantial than we are, the saint seeks littleness and dependence on God. We seek to find identity in the illusion of the false self that we create and hope other will confirm as our identity. Our real self, however, lies not in the facade of who we would like others to think we are, but in who we really are at the core of our being. This self is what the saint has discovered, and to which the saint constantly returns through repentance. It is the self that remains when all else is stripped away. Indeed, when all else is stripped away, we are no more than God's creation—God's beloved daughters and sons.

The way we come to this core of who we really are is always a way of descent. In contrast to the ladder of success that our culture tells us we should climb, the saint's journey is a downward journey through repentance. Indeed, we enter heaven as we descend into the littleness of the child who is nothing more than the object of their parent's love.[11] This will be our heavenly state, but the saint, unlike the rest of us, desires to live as close as possible to that state now. The way the saint achieves this is by living in a constant state of returning in repentance to the awareness of God's presence that is prayer.

11. Mark 10:15; Luke 18:17.

12

Theology in the Twenty-First Century

TODAY, WE HAVE COME to a point in our history where we realize that what we have traditionally dubbed *reality* is an interpretation of the data of our experience. Furthermore, we now know that the understanding through which we create our interpretation is not God-given, but comes to us at our mother's knee and is largely the product of human judgments passed onto us through our history, culture, and language communities. Thus, if we are serious about following Jesus, we must rethink much of our inherited understanding in the light of what Jesus said and did. In order to get a more transparent interpretation of the gospel, we need to be suspicious of the prejudices that make up our understanding, and allow the things that Jesus said and did to change that understanding.

Jesus disciples constantly had to rethink the understanding through which they were interpreting Jesus' radical teachings. Their misinterpretation was always a result of the fact that their understanding was inadequate to interpret what Jesus was saying and doing. The same is true concerning the history of Jesus followers down to our present day. Over the last two thousand years, people who were serious about following Jesus have allowed his teachings and life to change their understanding. The purpose of all such changes is to bring us to a more transparent interpretation of the gospel. Sadly, the religious establishment meets all such changes with opposition. Their opposition is always rooted in the same erroneous belief that the understanding or perspective of the religious establishment was sacred. In fact, however, it is God that is sacred, and not our understanding or perspective. We all too easily make an idol of our understanding and our theology becomes the thing in which we place our faith and trust. We believe that it rather than God will save us, and faith becomes simply a matter of having the right understanding.

In the past, such idolatrous faith in our own understanding had murderous effects. People killed one another in the name of Jesus because they thought they were defending the gospel rather than a historically and culturally relative perspective of the gospel. Fortunately, we now know that our understanding of everything, including the gospel, is perspectival and what we most often defend is our ego's attachment to that perspective rather than the gospel itself. Our egos and their attachment to what we claim we know is what so often fuels our religious fervor. It is our perspective—which we mistake for truth—that often is the very thing that keeps us from the fullness of life to which God calls us.

The fullness of life God has for us in Christ Jesus requires that we renew our minds[1] and take on the mind of Christ.[2] In other words, we need to take on the Jesus perspective. Only as our understanding comes closer to replicating Jesus' understanding do we begin to get a more transparent interpretation of Jesus and the gospel. Unfortunately, there is a great obstacle: we tend to believe that our theological understanding represents who God is, and we therefore treat that understanding as if it were some absolute truth rather than simply our understanding or perspective.

In other areas, apart from theology, we are better at adapting new perspectives. Most of us do not have much trouble understanding that Albert Einstein offers a better perspective of the physical universe than did Isaac Newton. Likewise, we find it easy to understand that a psychologist at the beginning of the twenty-first century does not have the same perspective on the human psyche that Freud had at the beginning of the twentieth century. We accept the idea that historically our perspective and understanding of the world and our place in it changes. With new discoveries and insights, our understanding changes and opens new vistas not available in the past. Philosophy and science are generally open to such new perspectives, although usually not without some resistance. Theology, on the other hand, confronts such new perspectives with more

1. Rom. 12:2.
2. Phil 2:5.

than a little resistance. Many people, who can accept Einstein's perspective in physics or a twenty-first-century perspective concerning the human psyche, insist upon retaining an unaltered sixteenth-century theology, in spite of the better understanding that the last 500 years has produced. Their defense is that God has not changed. But the physical universe and human psyche have not changed either. What has changed is our understanding of them. The change is the result of discoveries and insights that give us a better perspective. Luther and Calvin, as well as those of the Counter-Reformation, believed that the sun went around the earth rather than the earth going around the sun. They thought that was what they saw. We now know, however, that it was the result of their biased perspective, which imagined that the sun was moving and not the earth. We have a better perspective today. Why then should we not equally be open to a better perspective of the gospel than what was available previously?

We no longer believe that the sun goes around the earth because that is what we see, nor do we believe that when we read a text our interpretation is a result of what we see in that text. The theologians of the Reformation did believe such things. They believed that their interpretation of the gospel was no interpretation at all but the result of what they saw in the text. Today we know that what we think we see is not simply the result of what is there but largely determined by what we bring to our experience. The world that we experience is phenomenal or hermeneutical; that is, a composite of both the raw data of experience and what we bring to that data. What we bring in terms of the understanding that forms our interpretation of the data are concepts that are the product of human judgments passed onto us by our history, culture, and language communities. Thus, we all possess a very *human* perspective, and none of us has a God's-eye view. We may have some God-given concepts but most of what makes up the understanding through which we interpret the world is of a human origin. Thus, we are interpretative beings, and our interpretive nature is what separates us from the rest of nature. Without history, culture, or language other creatures may interpret the data of their experience largely through a God-given understanding, but human beings certainly do not. With what we now know concerning the nature of the understanding through which we interpret our experience, we should be more suspicious of that understanding and the way that it prejudices all of our experiences.

In the past, when we imagined that the mind was a *tabula rasa*, and we simply recorded data as given, hermeneutics or the study of interpretation had little place in our lives. It was the province of scholars seeking to interpret obscure texts. Unlike past generations who naively supposed that the way we conceptualized the world was the way the world was, we now understand the hermeneutical nature of our human condition. Today, we know that our human experience is a "text" that we must read and interpret.

Many see this perspectival and interpretive nature of our human condition as a threat to their faith and wish for an earlier time when we believed that our experience was simply something we received as given, instead of an interpretive process to which we add so much. The reason this is so threatening to so many is that they conceive of faith as a matter of believing certain propositions they hold to be true. Historically, the reformers idea of faith eventually came to mean that one believed doctrines different from those of Catholics, just as Catholic faith came to mean believing in doctrines and creeds different from what Protestants believed. Of course, the propositions that form our theological doctrines and creeds depend upon words, which we now know are not God-given. Human language has its content determined by forces at work within history, culture, and language communities. Hence, the words that constituted the propositional doctrines in which our modern ancestors put their faith reflected more our historical, cultural, and linguistic perspective rather than divine truths. Thus, faith became a matter of believing in one's own understanding, which was naively taken for truths concerning God. Consequently, Protestants killed Catholics and Catholics killed Protestants all in the name of God, because they imagined that their understanding represented objective truths about God. In the past, it was much easier for human beings to imagine that their understanding somehow reflected objective, sacred truths. Thankfully, we now know that the understanding through which we interpret God's communion with us is human rather than divine.

THE NATURE OF FAITH

Faith is certainly essential to most religious traditions, and we read that "without faith, it is impossible to please God."[3] For many people, however, a Christian faith means that they believe that Jesus was the Son of God, born of a virgin, rose from the dead, and is the second person of the Trinity. Of course, biblical faith, and especially the faith that Jesus speaks of in the Gospels, is very different from that. As we have seen, on the two occasions where Jesus praises people for having great faith, neither involves individuals who believed the right sacred facts, hold the appropriate doctrines, or are members of the right religious group. They were rather people who had discovered some deep truth concerning the nature of God through the circumstances of their lives. The Roman centurion knew something about divine authority. As a Roman commander, he was in a position of authority in Palestine, and a Jew like Jesus was under his authority, but this Roman centurion had come to know what real authority was. He knew that he had authority only because he was under the authority of Rome and he recognized that Jesus was under an even great authority than that of Rome.[4] Regarding the Syrophenician woman who Jesus tells us had great faith, we know that she is not of the right religious group, and all we know about what she believed was that she had come to discover that God took care of even the dogs that eat from the table.[5] That was enough for Jesus to tell us that she was a woman of great faith. Both these people had beliefs that shaped their understanding in ways that were conducive to their coming to know God, and who they were in relationship to God.

What we believe is certainly important but what is important is that our beliefs bring us to a better understanding of who God is and who we are in relationship to God. The Pharisees of Jesus' day had a religious faith that did just the opposite. They had a pride and confidence in their own understanding that closed them to the great understanding Jesus was offering.

By contrast, in the two instances above which Jesus calls great faith, both people had a humility that opened them to the possibility of God

---

3. Heb 11:6.

4. Luke 7:2–10.

5. Matt 15:21–28; Mark 7:24–30.

bringing them to an ever-greater understanding through which to interpret their God-experiences. The Roman centurion was in a place of authority, but rather than that creating a pride and confidence within him, it humbled him because he understood that his authority came from being under the greater authority of Rome. Likewise, the Syrophenician woman was also humble enough to receive the revelation of God's mercy through dogs eating from the scraps of the table. Both were open to receiving God's revelation through the circumstances of their lives in ways that the Pharisees were not. The only authority the Pharisees were under was their own understandings of the Law, and therefore they were unable to recognize that Jesus was under a greater authority, and, of course, they were also too proud to be taught by dogs.

Today, we should be in a better place than many of the religious people of Jesus' day, since we now know that there is nothing sacred about our understanding and the interpretation it yields. Perhaps past generations of Christians, like the Pharisees, found it easy to believe that their beliefs and understanding represented some objective, sacred truth, but we are not so naive today. Because of what we now know concerning the phenomenal or hermeneutical nature of our human experience, we should no longer be in a place of treating our own understanding with such reverence. This should open us to having our understanding changed by the things that Jesus said and did. We dub the process by which we come to that better understanding, "the hermeneutic circle."

THE HERMENEUTIC CIRCLE

The hermeneutic circle is the means to a more transparent interpretation. It begins with a suspicion concerning the understanding we bring to our experience. Without such a suspicion, we take the interpretation that our understanding creates as synonymous with the data of our experience. By doing so, our interpretation becomes irremediable and it, rather than God, becomes the thing in which we place our faith and trust. Without a healthy suspicion of our own understanding, there is no spiritual journey into the great mystery of God's mercy. Without a suspicion of our own understanding, we, like the Pharisees of Jesus' day, suffer no self-doubt and are convinced that our understanding is adequate to interpret all we need to know concerning God and our relationship to him. By contrast,

Jesus disciples, and all those who have truly decided to follow Jesus for the last two thousand years, have always been people who did not trust in their own understanding but were open to the Jesus revelation changing that understanding. If faith is to produce an ever-greater understanding of God and ourselves, we must be like those followers of Jesus who had enough humility to suppose that their understanding with which they first encounter God is insufficient. It is only through a general suspicion or distrust concerning our understanding that we become open to having God change our understanding in order to bring us to an ever more fruitful interpretation.

By supposing that our understanding is always insufficient or that a "non-understanding is never eliminated,"[6] we open ourselves to future readings, which are always worthwhile if we bring an openness to those readings. By allowing the Gospel texts to change our understanding, future readings are readings with a new understanding, which can produce more transparent and fruitful interpretations. Without openness to having our understanding corrected, future readings simply further confirm the prejudices that constitute our understanding, and their worth is only to reassure our egos of their rightness.

Of course, such openness could at times produce an understanding that yields a less transparent interpretation, but God can work with that and correct that misunderstanding as long as we stay open to having our understanding corrected. The point is not to be right and not make mistakes, but to stay on the journey and allow God to continue to draw us into an ever more fruitful understanding through which to interpret our God-experiences.

This is the nature of the hermeneutic circle. It is a dialogue, in which we allow the text to correct our understanding and thereby provide new ways to conceptualize what we experience in the text. This should be our means of reading any worthwhile text or experience but it is especially appropriate for some ultimately worthwhile texts like the Gospels. Unfortunately, this is not a very common practice. The way most read something like the Sermon on the Mount is with very little suspicion concerning the understanding they bring to that text. They think their

---

6. Schleiermacher, "Über den Begriff der Hermeneutik," In *Hermeneutik und Kritik*, edited by M. Frank, 328. Frankfurt: Suhrkamp, 1977. Quoted in Grondin, *Introduction*, 70.

understanding is adequate, and consequently they have no great expectation of the text changing that understanding. They simply read it in a way that confirms all the prejudices they bring to the reading. If, however, they would allow the radical teachings of Jesus to change their understanding, then the next reading of that text will be with a new understanding, which, in turn, will produce a new and hopefully a more transparent interpretation.

The spiritual journey into a more transparent interpretation of the gospel requires a great faith in the gospel and an equally great distrust toward our own understanding. Only then do we allow the text to do its job of changing our understanding in order to provide that deeper interpretation. This is what made the disciplines of Jesus different from the Pharisees. The religious people of Jesus' day knew what they knew and nothing could change their understanding, which they mistook for sacred. Jesus' disciples, on the other hand, were constantly having their understanding challenged and changed by the things Jesus said and did. If this was the kind of open faith to which Jesus called his disciples, then the very thing that keeps us from such a faith is the idea that faith is a matter of tenaciously clinging to a fixed and certain understanding. If we are truly to be followers of Jesus, the spiritual journey he calls us to will always challenge our understanding rather than reassure it. This is the nature of a spiritual journey and the nature of the hermeneutic circle as well. Both require that we hold our understanding loosely in order that our ongoing God-experiences change our understanding in order to give us a better interpretation. As we have said, what we are after is not objective truth. Even if we did have access to objective truth, how would it benefit us? What does benefit us is the Jesus perspective. What we want is to interpret the circumstances of our lives through the understanding that Jesus provides. This is what equips us for the spiritual journey. The religious establishment of Jesus' day failed to realize the nature of the spiritual journey to which Jesus was calling them, and likewise, much of today's religious establishment fails to realize it as well.

All this is not to say that the initial understanding we bring to the data of our experience is unimportance. Without our initial understanding, wrong as it may be, we would have no orientation to the data at all. Without some kind of understanding, it would be difficult to extract any meaning from the Gospel text. Our initial understanding gives us an orientation and tells us what is important and what is not important. When we were children, our parents and others oriented us by explaining what was important to focus on and what was not so important. When crossing a street some lights were important and some were not important. The red light that controlled the flow of traffic was important, and the street light that illumined the area was not something that we had to focus upon. We learned to focus on and highlight certain parts of our experience and ignore other parts. If we were to take in everything without some orientation that allowed us to sort and prioritize things, life would be very difficult. As useful as this orientation is, however, we all too quickly come to imagine that the interpretation it provides represents an objective reality rather than a specific interpretation.

One of the great problems with following Jesus is that we all too easily come to take our initial orientation of the gospel as synonymous with the gospel itself. Therefore, we end up worshipping and trusting our initial understanding rather than allowing the gospel to draw us into the journey that brings us to know the great mystery that is God. Idolatry or worshipping something other than God has always been the great sin, perhaps it is the only sin, but it assumes many disguises that often make it hard to recognize as sin. The most deceptive disguise has always been that of religion, whereby religious doctrines masquerade as God. Thankfully, today this particular idolatry has been unmasked. We now know that we are interpretive beings, and that our historical, cultural, and linguistic perspective limits that interpretation. None of us can claim a God's-eye view. We perceive things from within our particular journey and not from the perspective of eternity, as does God. Thus, the words of our religious doctrines may create metaphors that point toward God, but they can never adequately express the nature of an infinite and eternal God.

The best that true Christian religion can offer is an orientation or initial understanding that sets us on our spiritual journey. As we spend time in God's presence, our understanding is changed and we come to a better interpretation of the things that Jesus said and did. The journey brings us into a more transparent understanding; that is, one that reflects less our history, culture, and linguistic tradition, and is more reflective of Jesus' own perspective. Furthermore, the more we take on the Jesus' perspective, the better we are equipped to follow him and thereby become evermore like him.

Of course, it is difficult to stay on such a journey. We all too easily fall prey to gnosticism, and after God changes our understanding a bit, we imagine that we now know all there is to know. We find great security in the sense that *we know*, and we choose to rest there rather than to continue on the journey. In order to remain on the journey into an ever-greater perspective from which to better interpret the gospel and the fullness of life God has for us, we constantly need to seek that place of deep prayer. The reason prayer is so essential to staying on the journey is because there is a security that comes from sensing God's presence in prayer that allows us to let go of the false security that our own understanding provides.

A spiritual journey always requires that we see our present understanding as insufficient, but if people only find security in being certain about what they know, they will never let go of that understanding. In order to abandon the security we have in our understanding we must find a security apart from that understanding. The awareness of God's presence that we experience in deep prayer provides that security. It provides that peace that passes all understanding,[7] and provides a security that our understanding never can. "And the peace of God, which surpasses all understanding, will guard your hearts and minds in Christ Jesus."[8]

OUR HERMENEUTICAL NATURE AND THE BIBLICAL REVELATION

We now know that we are interpretive beings and an objective understanding of anything, least of all an infinite and eternal God, is beyond us. Although we have only recently become aware of our hermeneutical nature, our human condition has always been hermeneutical and our history has always progressed through a hermeneutical circle. Unlike other creatures, we human beings have a history because our understanding changes over time and produces different interpretations of our experience. Copernicus came to conceptualize his experience of the heavens differently than Ptolemy and he passed his understanding and interpretation on to us. Likewise, Albert Einstein had a different understanding of the physical universe than Isaac Newton and we are the heirs of Einstein's understanding and interpretation. In the same way, Jesus offers a better

7. Phil 4:7.
8. Ibid.

understanding through which to interpret our God-experience than any understanding that had come before him.

Since we are hermeneutical creatures and we have a history because of our hermeneutical nature, it seems obvious that the biblical revelation would depict this hermeneutical and historical nature of our human condition. I believe the Bible is God's infallible revelation, but what God is revealing is how human beings experience God through their all too human understanding. As such, the biblical revelation is a progressive revelation because it begins in a great misunderstanding, since our finite and temporal human understanding is ill equipped to interpret experiences with an infinite and eternal God. This infinite and eternal God, however, patiently works amid our misunderstanding in order to bring us to a better understanding, and eventually to the ultimate perspective, which is the Jesus revelation.

Sadly, such a view meets with great opposition from a modern form of Gnosticism. As we said earlier, Gnosticism is the great heresy that has always plagued religion. In its modern form, Gnosticism insisted that our knowledge of God be objective, certain, and precise, but that is part of an unholy desire to know as God knows. The eternal temptation that takes us out of a right place of humility before God is to believe the lie that we can know as God knows. We first believed that lie in the Garden,[9] but we are finally in a place where we can see it for the lie that it is. Our knowing will forever be an interpretation from our limited perspective, but as we stay humble and open, God can change our understanding in order to give us a more transparent interpretation of our God-experiences. The greatest opposition to this openness has always come from a religious establishment that claims to know all they need to know. The religious leaders of Galileo's day insisted that they knew with objective certainty that the sun revolves around the earth. Objective certainty has always attracted religious types but it is antithetical to any genuine spiritual journey.

A genuine spiritual journey always requires openness to the better understanding God has for us. The religious establishment is always opposed to such openness, so God usually works through the religious outsider. The founders of most religious orders, like the Protestant reformers, and the desert fathers, were all initially either heretics or outsiders to their religious establishment. God has to work through the religious outsider

9. Gen 3:1–5.

because the religious establishment is always trying to protect the false security that comes from the understanding they set forth as sacred, while God is always trying to bring us to a better understanding.

Just as our intellectual history is progressive because individual scholars defy the interpretation of their day and introduce a new understanding through which a more transparent interpretation is possible, the Jewish prophets, all the way down to John the Baptist and Jesus, similarly defy the religious establishment of their day. The Scripture is a progressive revelation for the same reason that our intellectual history is progressive; that is, there is, in the development of human consciousness, an ongoing awareness that there is a better understanding through which to interpret our experience. This is what makes for the historicity of our human condition. Unlike the rest of nature, we are a historical species that are capable of changing the understanding through which we interpret the world. Since we now know this about our human condition, it should not be surprising that the biblical revelation is God's revelation of this historical and hermeneutical nature of our relationship with God. Since we now know that we are interpretative beings and our interpretation changes over the course of time, how could the biblical revelation be anything but God's revelation of how human beings have interpreted their relationship with God? As such, it is the revelation of how God patiently works within the development of human consciousness to bring us to a better understanding through which to interpret our God experiences.

People who are on a genuine spiritual journey should have little problem accepting such a view of Scripture since it mirrors what they have experienced in their own personal relationship with God. With our first God-experiences, like those first experiences depicted in the biblical revelation, we almost all begin with an understanding of a wrathful and punishing God who must be appeased. God's desire, however, is that we would eventually come to interpret our God-experiences through an understanding of God as a loving father who desires mutual indwelling. That is the perfect understanding of God's love that casts out all fear.[10]

Of course, we only come to such a different interpretation of our God-experience if we are open to having our understanding changed. Most of us are open to having our understanding changed, at least to some degree. We are able to adapt to the new understandings that Copernicus

10. 1 John 4:18.

and Einstein offer. As long as the changes are not too drastic and they do not impact our lives too much, we can accommodate them and reinterpret the world through such a new understanding. When we encounter an understanding too drastic, however, we simply reject it as radical and too far from the norm to be something we can use in order to create a viable interpretation for ourselves. Unfortunately, the understanding that the Jesus revelation offers is just such an understanding. The Jesus perspective does not offer a modification to our understanding the way that Copernicus or Einstein had, but it threatens to obliterate it and replace it with something so divinely alien that we baulk—it is simply too much for us.

THE JESUS REVELATION

The Jesus revelation is so radical that rather than accept it as the ultimate perspectival understanding from which to interpret our experiences with God, we fall back upon theories that suppress the Jesus revelation. We adopt a theory about all of Scripture being the objective revelation of who God is in order that the words of Jesus must conform to the rest of Scripture. We insist upon imagining that the Scripture is a revelation of God's objective nature, in order that the Jesus revelation is no different from the revelations of Moses and David. We want to believe that all of Scripture is a revelation of who God objectively is so we can balance the words of Jesus with the rest of Scripture. Thus, when Jesus tells us to love our enemies in order that we might be like God who is "kind to the ungrateful and the wicked,"[11] we can point to other portions of Scripture where God seems to be telling us to kill our enemies.[12] Whenever Jesus says something too radically divine for us, we reference another Scripture that says the very opposite. We suppress the words of Jesus by making his words conform to the rest of Scripture, instead of making the rest of Scripture conform to his words. We do this so we can imagine that sometimes what Jesus says is the prescription for our lives but something God's prescription is just the opposite. This gives us the option of deciding whether this is a time for loving our enemies or killing our enemies.

When the words of Jesus contradict other portions of Scripture, we who consider ourselves Christians almost always side against the words of

11. Luke 6:35.
12. Josh 6:21.

Jesus. When Jesus says, "Whoever comes to me and does not hate father and mother, wife and child, brother and sister, yes, even life itself, cannot be my disciple,"[13] we quickly point to other portions of Scripture in order to show that Jesus did not really mean what he said. Instead of treating the words of Jesus as sacred, it is our theory about God's revelation being a revelation of objective reality that we hold as sacred. Thankfully, today a belief that objective reality is something to which we have access is indefensible and we can no longer use such a theory to suppress the words of Jesus.

With such a theory debunked, we are now free to see the Jesus revelation as the ultimate understanding through which we should interpret our God-experiences. Jesus' interpretation of his God-experiences should provide the benchmark by which we can determine whether other portions of Scripture represent a more or less transparent interpretation of the God-experiences recorded there. Simply put, the portions of Scripture that conform to the gospel are the better interpretations of God's communion with human beings, and those that oppose what the gospel reveals are interpretation formed out of a more human and less divine understanding.

Of course, some continue to believe that God can bypass the understanding through which we process our experience and give us purely objective revelations—that is, experiences that are all God and nothing of us. Since we now know that God did not do that with the natural revelation, and we do not see the sun going around the earth, as we once believed, why would we believe that the Scripture is an objective revelation? I think the answer to that question is twofold. First, it gives religious people a way to neutralize the Jesus revelation by making the revelations of Moses, Joshua, or David as much a revelation of God's nature as the revelation that Jesus offers. We much prefer the more human interpretations offered in other parts of Scripture rather than the radically divine interpretation that Jesus' understanding offers. Since we much prefer the more human interpretation, we cling to theories of interpretation that suppress the Jesus revelation. We cling to theories that insist that the words and deeds of Jesus conform to the rest of Scripture, instead of understanding the rest of Scripture in the context of everything that Jesus said and did. By making a theory about objectivity sacred rather than Jesus, we can believe

13. Luke 14:26.

that sometimes God wants us to kill our enemies rather than love them. No wonder we cling to the idea of objectivity so desperately.

The second reason we love and defend the idea of objective God-experiences, which are pure God and nothing of us, is that they provides fragile egos who wish to suffer no self-doubt with a sense of certainty. If God imparts objective truths to them, they can have the confidence in their own understanding that their egos crave. The faith that Jesus calls us to, however, is very different. Rather than offering certainty for our understanding and stability for our egos, the Jesus revelation does violence to our understanding and destabilizes our egos. In order to follow Jesus we must learn to hold our interpretation loosely and trust not in our own understanding,[14] but allow the gospel to change our understanding and bring us to a more transparent interpretation of what Jesus is revealing.

As we have said, this is not easy to do. Without that experience of God's presence and the peace and security it offers, we inevitably seek security in our own understanding and insist upon its certainty. A security in the certainty of our own understanding is something we can own and possess. It gives us a sense of power that gratifies the ego, but the truth that Jesus offers is neither the certainty we crave nor an understanding that we can easily grasp. It is something we never possess but it possesses us. It is not something we can get a hold of but something that gets a hold of us. It is something that is always out beyond that draws us deeper and deeper into a mystery that we only come to know as we spend time in God's presence. Without the experience of God's presence and the mystery of his mercy, which we come to know through that presence, we will always look to our own understanding for security and to the theological gods we create in order to provide our egos with the certainty they crave.

14. Prov 3:5.

Bibliography

Anselm. *Anselm of Canterbury: The Major Works*. Edited by Brian Davies and G. R. Evans. New York: Oxford University Press, 1998.

Augustine. *De Magistro*. In *Augustine: Earlier Writings*, edited and translated by John H. S. Burleigh, 64–101. The Library of Christian Classics 6. Philadelphia, PA: Westminster, 1953.

Brother Lawrence of the Resurrection. *The Practice of the Presence of God*. Translated by John J. Delaney. New York: Doubleday, 1975.

Edwards, Jonathan. *The Religious Affections*. Carlisle, PA: Banner of Truth, 1997.

Ehman, Robert. "Personal Love." In *Eros, Agape, and Philia: Readings in the Philosophy of Love*, edited by Alan Soble, 254–72. New York: Paragon, 1989.

Grondin, Jean. *Introduction to Philosophical Hermeneutics*. Translated by Joel Weinsheimer. New Haven, CT: Yale University Press, 1994.

Hick, John. *Evil and the God of Love*. 2nd ed. New York: Harper & Row, 1977.

Nouwen, Henri. *Encounters with Merton*. New York: Crossroad, 1981.

Ortega y Gasset, Jose. *On Love: Aspects of a Single Theme*. Translated by Toby Talbot. New York: Penguin, 1957.

Tenney, Tommy. *The God Chasers*. Shippensburg, PA: Destiny Image, 1998.

Weaver, Denny J. "Violence in Christian Theology." *Cross Currents* 51.2 (2001). Online: http://www.crosscurrents.org/weaver0701.htm.

Index

abortion, 69–70
affection, degrees of, 17
anger
  causing lack of awareness of God's
    presence, 66–67
  as god and source of energy, 58
Anselm, 74
anxiety, as source of energy, 61
Aristotle, 110
atonement theory, 75
attention
  as base of love, 14
  focusing of, 14–15
  God's provision of, 15
Augustine, 107
  on Jesus' instructions for prayer,
    36–37
  on words being unnecessary for
    prayer, 24

beatific vision, 107
Beatitudes, 63–65
being in love, 17–18, 20–21
Bible, journey motif in, 10
biblical revelation, progressive nature of,
    125, 126
born-again experience, 41, 68–69
Brother Lawrence, 5, 43

Calvin, John, 74, 117
Catherine of Genoa, 26
celebrity Christians, 108–9
certainty

antithetical to spiritual journey,
    125–26
  equated with truth, 10
Christianity
  about restoring relationship through
    forgiveness, 78
  unappealing nature of, 78
Christus Victor, 73–74
communication, as being present for
    another, 24–25
consciousness, experiencing the presence
    of another, 26
contemplative prayer
  being present to God in, 42
  distinguished from religious prayer,
    37
  maximizing the experience of
    forgiveness, 79
  mystery of, xiii
  practice of, 39–40, 43
  purpose of, 43
  suspending understanding through,
    42
control, xiv, xv, 39
Copernicus, 124
cultural anthropology, 2

dark night of the soul, 11–12
Dewey, John, 6–7
disciples
  called to open faith, 122
  misinterpretations of, 115
Eastern religions, growing in popularity,
    9

Index

Eckhart, Meister, 26
Edwards, Jonathan, 5–6
ego, attachment to, 116
Einstein, Albert, 2, 9, 116, 124
enemies, love of, 49, 60, 70
evil
    elimination of, through forgiveness,
        106
    God's tolerance for, 102–3
    as instrumental, 99
    opposition to, 104
    problem of, 98–99
Evil and the God of Love (Hick), 99–100
experience
    lacking in objectivity, 1–3
    phenomenal nature of, 2–3
    as text, 118

faith
    belief in theologies referred to as,
        21–22
    as believing one's own understanding,
        6, 118, 120, 123
    nature of, 119–20
falling in love, xiv, 14. *See also* God,
        falling in love with
false identity, 35
family values, 69–70
flesh, making forgiveness difficult, 50–51
flesh and spirit, metaphor of, 33–36
forgiveness, 30
    becoming aware of, 20, 47–48
    capacity for, 49, 50
    dependence on, 19–20
    eliminating evil through, 106
    experiencing, 12–13
    in the flesh, 51–52
    giving and receiving, 19
    greater than sin, 47
    leading to humility, 90
    maximizing, through contemplative
        prayer, 79
    meaning suffering the offense of
        others, 20
    receiving on a constant basis,
        awareness of, 100–101
    remorse not required for, 55

restoring relationship through, 77–78
satisfying justice, 77
seeing need for, 45–47
Francisco de Osuna, 5
Freeman, Lawrence, 42
Freud, Sigmund, 116
future, escaping the pull of, 24–25, 26

Gnosticism, 124, 125
God
    being in love with, 17–18, 20–21, 22,
        106–7
    being transformed into his likeness,
        48
    calling us to a life in prayer, 44–45
    calling us to relationship, 63
    continuing to suffer our rejection,
        101
    creating us in his image and likeness,
        19, 47–48
    desiring to restore relationship with
        us, 77
    developing a relationship with, 32
    falling in love with, xiv, 75–76
    fear of, 76
    having tolerance for evil, 102–3
    inside track to, 71
    listening to us listening to him, 24
    looking to, for security, 6
    love of, related to being attentive to
        his presence, 16–17
    love for us different than our love for
        each other, 88
    manifest presence of, 27–30
    mystery of, 4–5, 8–10
    nonpreferential love of, 19
    omnipresence of, 25–32
    people's awareness of his presence,
        27–29
    perfecting our moral behavior,
        99–100
    pleased with our presence, regardless
        of our behavior, 87–88
    practicing being aware of his
        presence, 39
    presence of, 11. *See also* God,
        omnipresence of

7539

DATE DUE

			PRINTED IN U.S.A.